P9-CQV-480

NORTH KOREA
in Pictures

Alison Behnke

Lerner Publications Company

Contents

Lerner Publishing Group realizes that current information and statistics quickly become out of date. To extend the usefulness of the Visual Geography Series, we developed www.vgsbooks.com, a website offering links to up-to-date information, as well as in-depth material, on a wide variety of subjects. All of the websites listed on www.vgsbooks.com have been carefully selected by researchers at Lerner Publishing Group. However, Lerner Publishing Group is not responsible for the accuracy or suitability of the material on any website other than <www.lernerbooks.com>. It is recommended that students using the Internet be supervised by a parent or teacher. Links on www.vgsbooks.com will be regularly reviewed and updated as needed.

Note to Readers: This book uses the McCune-Reischauer system of romanization for Korean proper nouns. Please see page 7 for more information.

Website address: www.lernerbooks.com

Lerner Publications Company
A division of Lerner Publishing Group
241 First Avenue North
Minneapolis, MN 55401 U.S.A.

web enhanced @ www.vgsbooks.com

CULTURAL LIFE   48

► Religion. Holidays and Festivals. Food and Dress. Visual Arts. Literature and Film. Music and Dance. Sports.

THE ECONOMY   58

► Industry and Trade. Military Spending and Weapons Production. Agriculture, Forestry, and Fishing. Service Sector. Infrastructure. The Future.

FOR MORE INFORMATION

Library of Congress Cataloging-in-Publication Data

Behnke, Alison.
        North Korea in pictures / by Alison Behnke.
            p.   cm. — (Visual geography series)
        Includes bibliographical references and index.
        ISBN: 0-8225-1908-9 (lib. bdg. : alk. paper)
        1. Korea (North)—Pictorial works—Juvenile literature. 2. Korea (North)—Juvenile literature. 3. Korea—Pictorial works—Juvenile literature. I. Title. II. Series.
        DS932.23.B44 2005
        951.93—dc22   2004013198

Manufactured in the United States of America
1 2 3 4 5 6 - JR - 10 09 08 07 06 05

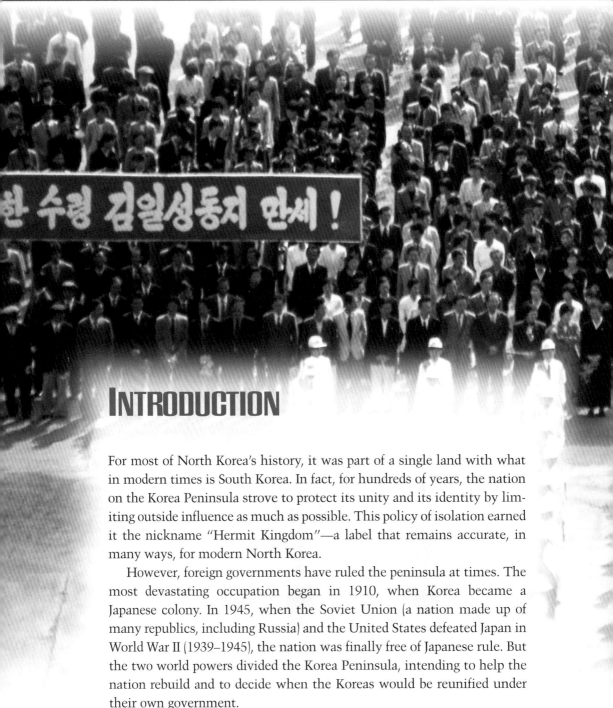

INTRODUCTION

For most of North Korea's history, it was part of a single land with what in modern times is South Korea. In fact, for hundreds of years, the nation on the Korea Peninsula strove to protect its unity and its identity by limiting outside influence as much as possible. This policy of isolation earned it the nickname "Hermit Kingdom"—a label that remains accurate, in many ways, for modern North Korea.

However, foreign governments have ruled the peninsula at times. The most devastating occupation began in 1910, when Korea became a Japanese colony. In 1945, when the Soviet Union (a nation made up of many republics, including Russia) and the United States defeated Japan in World War II (1939–1945), the nation was finally free of Japanese rule. But the two world powers divided the Korea Peninsula, intending to help the nation rebuild and to decide when the Koreas would be reunified under their own government.

Before long, the philosophies of the Communist Soviet Union and the capitalist, anti-Communist United States clashed. Communism is a

political and social model based on the idea that property should be state owned rather than private and that all citizens should have equal resources. Capitalism, based on ideas of free trade and individual property, conflicts with Communism, and this difference put Soviet goals for Korea at odds with U.S. wishes. As disagreement grew about how the peninsula should operate, the division of Korea dragged on. When the Korean War (1950–1953) erupted, it looked as though the division would last far longer than anyone had envisioned.

The peninsula's division separated millions of North Koreans from their relatives in the South, and those ties kept alive a strong desire for reunification among Koreans on both sides. But the two nations followed very different paths after the war. North Korea, under the guidance of the Soviet Union, created a Communist government and officially became the Democratic People's Republic of Korea (DPRK). North Korea set itself on a track to develop industry

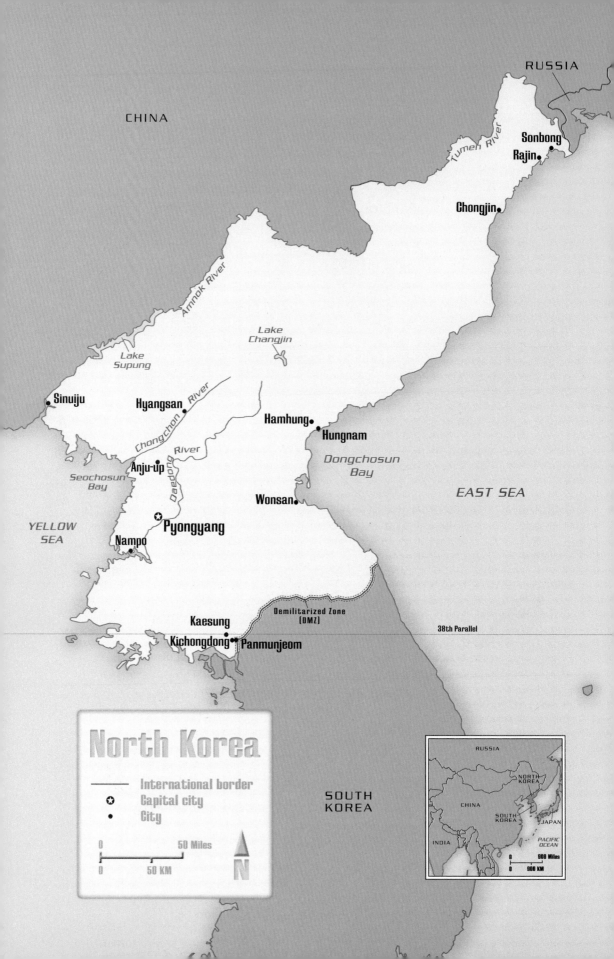

and agriculture rapidly. The nation was led by Kim Il Sung, a dictator around whom the government built a powerful cult of personality, raising him to almost divine status and urging all citizens to be entirely devoted to him. Meanwhile, South Korea embarked on a postwar plan embracing capitalism and democracy which, while sometimes rocky, resulted in many sharp contrasts between the modern Koreas.

With the collapse of the Soviet Union in 1991, North Korea lost much of its economic support. Further disaster struck with a series of crises including Kim Il Sung's death, devastating floods, and famine throughout the nation. These troubles were paired with a rising number of defections, as thousands of citizens risked their lives to leave the country illegally, most fleeing across the northern border to China. In addition, growing tensions with the United States and other

ALPHABET SOUP

When reading about Korea in various sources, you might notice that the same Korean name or word may be spelled in several different ways. These differences exist because two main methods are used for romanization (transferring Korean into the Roman alphabet used by English). These systems are the McCune-Reischauer and the newer Revised Romanization of Korean. Although South Korea has made Revised Romanization its official system, North Korea has chosen to continue using McCune-Reischauer. This book uses McCune-Reischauer.

nations over North Korea's suspected nuclear weapons program raised new challenges at the beginning of the twenty-first century. By 2004 the North Korean economy had slowly begun to recover, aided by gradually loosening restrictions and new openness to mild capitalist reform. These changes took place under Kim Il Sung's son Kim Jong-il. Nevertheless, North Korea's international relations remain deeply strained.

North Korea is a highly secretive nation whose leaders believe strongly in keeping the country closed to external influences, as well as in keeping hidden what goes on inside the nation. This isolation has led the nation to be misunderstood, mistrusted, and feared. At the same time, it allows the North Korean government to misrepresent the outside world to its own people. As this modern Hermit Kingdom moves into the future, it has many challenges ahead. But North Korea also has great resources to offer, from a rich history and culture to a deep national pride and an industrious population—resources that have, in some ways, been protected by many years of fierce privacy.

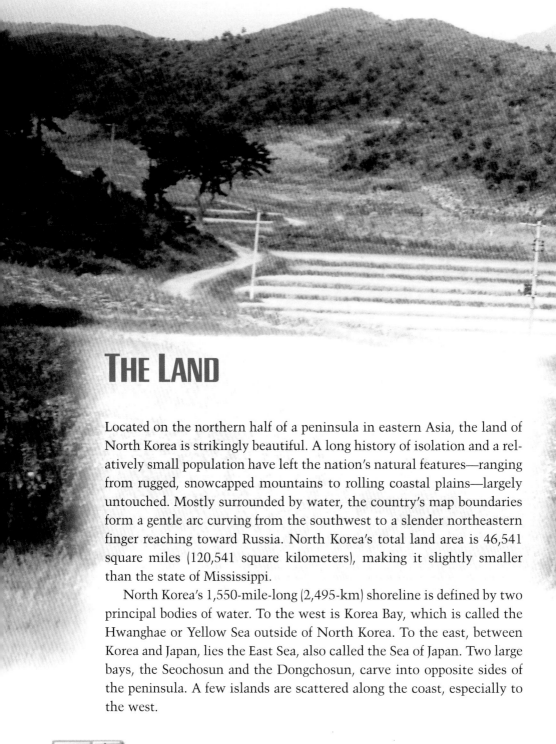

THE LAND

Located on the northern half of a peninsula in eastern Asia, the land of North Korea is strikingly beautiful. A long history of isolation and a relatively small population have left the nation's natural features—ranging from rugged, snowcapped mountains to rolling coastal plains—largely untouched. Mostly surrounded by water, the country's map boundaries form a gentle arc curving from the southwest to a slender northeastern finger reaching toward Russia. North Korea's total land area is 46,541 square miles (120,541 square kilometers), making it slightly smaller than the state of Mississippi.

North Korea's 1,550-mile-long (2,495-km) shoreline is defined by two principal bodies of water. To the west is Korea Bay, which is called the Hwanghae or Yellow Sea outside of North Korea. To the east, between Korea and Japan, lies the East Sea, also called the Sea of Japan. Two large bays, the Seochosun and the Dongchosun, carve into opposite sides of the peninsula. A few islands are scattered along the coast, especially to the west.

Most of North Korea's northern land boundary is with China, and a short stretch also borders Russia in the far northeast. To the south lies the Republic of Korea, or South Korea. Since the Korean War ended in 1953, the two Koreas have been separated at the Military Demarcation Line, near the 38th Parallel of latitude. A Demilitarized Zone (DMZ) patrolled by North Korean, South Korean, and U.S. soldiers, extends 1.2 miles (1.9 km) on each side of the border. Because North Korea hopes to reunify the peninsula eventually, it regards the line as temporary.

Topography

The most striking feature of North Korea's landscape is its dramatic mountains, which make up approximately 80 percent of the nation's area. The highest elevations are concentrated in the northeastern part of the country in the Hamgyong and Nangnim ranges. Along the border with China, the extinct volcano Baekdusan (also called Mount Baekdu)—the highest peak on the Korea Peninsula—juts out of the landscape, towering 9,020 feet (2,749 meters) above sea level. Koreans consider the mountain sacred and revere it as the birthplace of Korea's mythological founder, Dan-gun.

One of Korea's oldest and most treasured legends tells of Dan-gun and his founding of ancient Korea. According to the stories, Dan-gun himself was the son of a heavenly prince who came to earth and a bear that the prince transformed into a maiden.

Out of central North Korea rise the Myohyang Mountains, home to the peak Myohyangsan. At a height of more than 6,200 feet (1,890 meters), it is the site of beautiful hiking trails, Buddhist temples, museums, and modern hotels, making the spot a favorite for visitors. Many other ranges also stretch across the mountainous nation, and prominent peaks in northern and central North Korea include Kwanmobong (8,331 ft, or 2,539 m), Puksubaeksan (8,266 ft, or 2,519 m), and Nangnimsan (7,170 ft, or 2,185 m). Farther south and near the eastern coast, the horizon is dominated by the Taebaek Mountains, which reach southward across the border and into South Korea.

In eastern North Korea, the mountains plunge steeply to the sea. However, in the southwest, the mountains descend more gradually into hills and valleys that slope down to lowland plains along the coast of the Yellow Sea. Most of the nation's people live in these more hospitable lowlands. Local farmers grow the vast majority of the nation's crops in this region of rolling hills and plains, as the central and northeastern mountains are too rugged to support extensive agriculture.

◉ Rivers and Lakes

Most of North Korea's major rivers originate in the nation's numerous mountain ranges and flow westward, emptying into the Yellow Sea. The longest waterway, the Amnok (also known by the Chinese name Yalu), rises from the rugged northern borderlands and flows westward along the border with China for most of its 501 miles (806 km) before finally emptying into the Yellow Sea. The 245-mile-long (394-km-long) Daedong, which also empties into the Yellow Sea, begins in the Myohyang range.

Other major rivers include the Chongchon (in western North Korea) and the Tumen. While the Tumen is the nation's second-longest river at 324 miles (521 km), it flows through such mountainous territory in northeastern North Korea before reaching the East Sea that it is only navigable for about one-tenth of that length. The volume of water carried by North Korea's rivers varies widely, due to

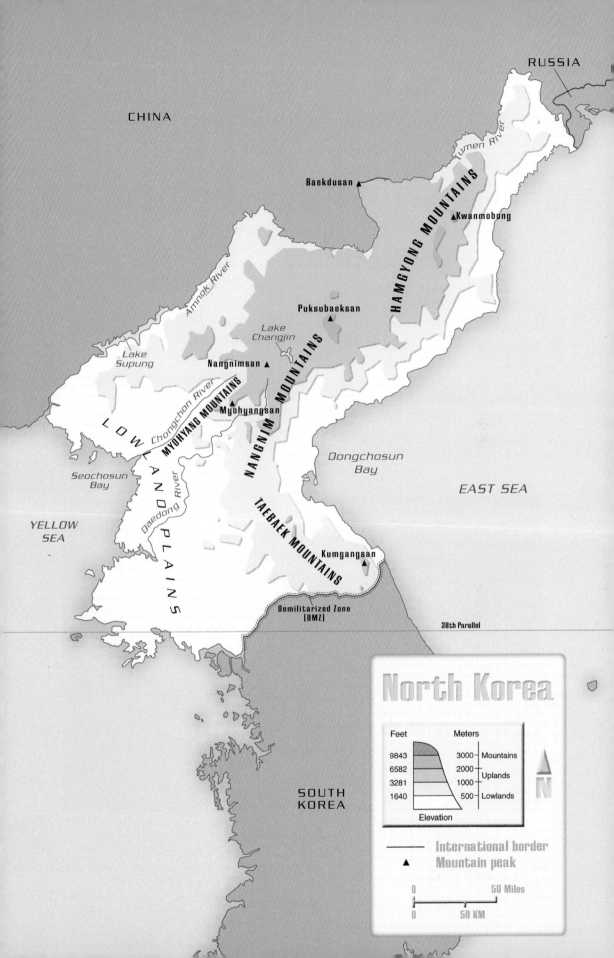

RUSSIA

CHINA

Tumen River

▲Baekdusan

HAMGYONG MOUNTAINS

▲Kwanmobong

Amnok River

Puksubaeksan ▲

Lake Changjin

Lake Supung

Nangnimsan ▲

NANGNIM MOUNTAINS

Chongchon River

MYOHYANG MOUNTAINS

▲ Myohyangsan

Dongchosun Bay

EAST SEA

Seochosun Bay

L O W L A N D   P L A I N S

Daedong River

YELLOW SEA

TAEBAEK MOUNTAINS

Kumgangsan ▲

Demilitarized Zone (DMZ)

38th Parallel

SOUTH KOREA

North Korea

Feet	Meters	
9843	3000	Mountains
6582	2000	Uplands
3281	1000	
1640	500	Lowlands

Elevation

N

——— International border
▲ Mountain peak

0   50 Miles

0   50 KM

HEAVENLY HEIGHTS

Like the mountain on which it rests, Cheonji, or Lake of Heaven, is deeply loved by Koreans, and it holds a special place in North Korean legend and lore. For example, stories of strange beasts living in the lake abound. On a more romantic note, popular tradition draws young couples to throw coins into the water, with the wish that their love will be as deep and lasting as the Cheonji itself.

distinct rainy and dry seasons. During the rainy season, large dams help control flooding. These dams also produce hydroelectric (water-fueled) power and regulate water for domestic and industrial uses. The nation's rivers are also important sources of irrigation, watering most of the nation's rice fields. A few small lakes also dot the landscape. They include Lake Supung, which is a widening of the Amnok River, and centrally located Lake Changjin. By far the most famous lake in North Korea is Cheonji, which fills a crater high on Baekdusan. With a maximum depth of 1,260 feet (384 m), the lake is one of the deepest—and coldest—in the world. Its surface of more than 3 square miles (7.8 sq. km) freezes over for much of the year, and few animals are hardy enough to survive in its waters.

A convoy of trucks crosses the **Tumen River.** The vehicles are carrying international medical aid and food packages into North Korea from China. Go to www.vgsbooks.com for links to learn more about North Korea's geography and wildlife.

Natural Resources and Environmental Challenges

North Korea's rivers serve as some of the nation's most valuable resources, supplying water for hydroelectricity and irrigation. In contrast, the Korea Peninsula's mountainous topography means that it has a relatively small amount of land suitable for farming—a natural resource that the country needs badly, as it has suffered from severe food shortages.

But North Korea is rich in other resources. Its vast forests, though increasingly threatened by logging, have long been one of the nation's most valuable natural treasures. In addition, important mineral resources such as coal, manganese (used in making metal mixtures), iron ore, and uranium lie beneath the earth. North Korea also reports large offshore oil reserves of up to 10 billion tons (9.1 billion metric tons). However, due to economic challenges, these remain largely unexplored and unconfirmed by outside sources, and the nation continues to import petroleum for energy purposes.

North Korea's shortage of farmland and energy sources are, in many ways, closely tied to its environmental challenges. Historically, Japanese control, war, and the nation's postwar industrialization took their toll on the nation's environment. But ongoing problems include attempts to expand the limited amount of farmland by cutting down trees and by planting crops on hillsides. These efforts have led to deforestation and erosion, which in turn have contributed to flooding.

Industrial pollution, while generally localized around factories and plants—many of which no longer even operate—is a problem in some areas. The use of chemical fertilizers on farmland is also a concern. And due to widespread famine, wildlife populations are believed to have been severely depleted by people seeking food.

The nation has officially passed a number of laws intended to protect the environment, but, they are believed to be loosely enforced or largely ignored. Nevertheless, one built-in safety guard is North Korea's relatively small population and its large expanses of virtually uninhabitable land. Many environmentalists hope that the difficulty of developing these areas will help keep them safe.

Climate

Seasonal winds called monsoons are one of the greatest factors affecting North Korea's weather. In July and August, monsoons blowing from the south and southeast bring warm, humid air to the country. Summer temperatures in the nation's capital, Pyongyang, typically hover near a pleasant 75°F (24°C). Colder, drier weather arrives during the winter, with bitter winds that blow from Siberia (a northern region of Russia). Pyongyang's average January temperature is about 18°F (–8°C). However, in the far north and in North Korea's many mountains, winter temperatures drop much lower.

North Korea receives about 35 to 40 inches (89 to 102 centimeters) of precipitation per year. Most of this falls in the form of rain, primarily between June and September. However, precipitation levels and patterns vary throughout the country and from year to year. Snow falls more frequently farther north on the peninsula, as well as in the mountains. In addition, devastating droughts periodically occur, often with disastrous effects for local farmers. A few typhoons (Pacific hurricanes) usually pass over North Korea in late summer, bringing strong winds and heavy rains that can damage crops and homes.

Flora and Fauna

North Korea, much of it covered with thick forest, is home to a wide variety of plant life. Pine trees, firs, and deciduous (leaf-shedding) hardwoods such as oak, birch, cedar, maple, ash, and elm fill the nation's forests. Above the timberline (a mountain boundary beyond which trees cannot grow), the highest mountains support alpine vegetation—tough, hardy plants that can survive high altitudes and cold temperatures. More delicate flora appears in warmer regions, especially during the peak period for flowering plants in July. Camellias blossom in the southwest, and other flowering plants include rhododendron and azaleas.

Some of the most treasured flowers in North Korea are two named after the nation's leaders. Kim Il Sung is honored with the *Kimilsungia*, a type of orchid that is the national flower. The *Kimjongilia*, a type of peony, is dedicated to son Kim Jong-il. Thousands of these flowers are displayed for the Kims' birthdays.

Along with this vegetation, the forests and mountains of North Korea are home to a variety of animals, including large creatures such as the Siberian black bear and the endangered Amur leopard. Siberian tigers prowl the wilderness, sometimes making meals of the fierce wild boars in the area. Smaller animals include shrews, weasels, pikas (small mammals related to rabbits), and Amur gorals (horned, hoofed animals in the goat family). Many birds also make their homes in North Korea, especially in the dense forests on Baekdusan's slopes. Black grouse, hawk owls, and several varieties of woodpeckers are found, as well.

Additional local wildlife includes various kinds of reptiles, amphibians, and freshwater fish.

Cities

Most of North Korea's cities were devastated during the Korean War, but after the conflict's end, the country gradually began to recover and rebuild. Pyongyang, the country's capital, is its most populous and most important city.

PYONGYANG With an estimated population of slightly more than 3 million people, the North Korean capital of Pyongyang is by far the nation's largest city. Situated on the Daedong River about 25 miles (40 km) east of the Yellow Sea, the city serves as the cultural, economic, educational, and governmental center of the country. Its history as a capital dates back more than 1,500 years to A.D. 427, when it became the capital of the ancient kingdom

SAFE HAVEN

The DMZ that separates North and South Korea has a reputation as one of the most dangerous places in the world, due to the presence of heavily armed soldiers, hidden land mines, and a constant atmosphere of tension. However, it also has the distinction of being a sanctuary for endangered species. With access to the region strictly controlled, animals and birds can roam freely and largely undisturbed within the narrow strip of land. Some of the rare creatures who make their homes here include white-naped cranes, Chinese egrets, Amur leopards (*above*), and Asiatic black bears.

Koguryo. North Korean leaders also proclaim that the city holds the grave of Dan-gun, the legendary founder of the first Korean kingdom.

Although it remained an important city through the centuries, Pyongyang has been devastated many times in different conflicts. The first destruction was the result of a Japanese attack in 1592. Later attacks by Chinese and Manchu warriors reduced the city to rubble twice more. In the twentieth century, an estimated 75 percent of the city was destroyed in the Korean War.

After this last war ended in 1953, Pyongyang was rebuilt as a capital once more, this time as the capital of the Communist Democratic People's Republic of Korea. Several museums display exhibits on North Korean history, the Kim family, and other patriotic subjects, and Pyongyang is also home to Kim Il Sung University, the country's most prestigious higher-education institution. The city's modern architecture reflects Communist styles and ideas, and Pyongyang is filled with statues and monuments to Kim Il Sung and Kim Jong-il. Wide squares and large parks also dot the city, and a pair of fountains sends water shooting about 490 feet (149 m) into the air from the middle of the Daedong River.

A sculpture of the Chollima from Korean mythology (center)—a winged horse capable of traveling at high speeds over enormous distances—towers 139 feet (42 m) over Pyongyang. Completed in 1961, the monument symbolizes North Korea's rapid economic transformation after the Korean War.

One of Pyongyang's interesting features is its remarkable cleanliness, especially for such a large city. Very little traffic crowds the capital's streets, which are swept of litter and other trash early each morning and washed twice every week. In addition, although North Korea's official policy on the subject is not public, the city's population itself is said to be specifically chosen to live there. Representing the elite of North Korean society, only people who have a history of strongly supporting the government and the Communist Party are permitted to be residents. Other restrictions are also said to be in place, prohibiting people who are ill, disabled, or very elderly from living in the city. Bicycles are discouraged on the streets, and street vendors are forbidden. The result is a city that, while very orderly and attractive, does not accurately represent the more diverse North Korean population for whom it serves as the capital.

OTHER CITIES North Korea's second-largest city is Nampo, with an estimated population of about 730,000. This major port and shipping center lies on the western coast. Workers in this industrial city specialize in fields such as shipbuilding, glassmaking, copper refining, and other manufacturing areas.

Hamhung's more than 700,000 residents make it the nation's third-largest population center. This important industrial city produces goods such as textiles, machinery, and chemicals. Plants located here also refine oil and process food, and the region has working coal mines. Hamhung is also remembered as the birthplace of Yi Song-gye, founder of the powerful and long-lived Chosun dynasty.

Smaller North Korean cities include Chongjin, Wonsan, and Hyangsan. These provincial capitals serve as local marketplaces and administrative centers.

In Nampo, dancers and musicians entertain the crowd that has turned out to celebrate the fiftieth anniversary of the Korean Workers' Party (KWP).

HISTORY AND GOVERNMENT

As a historical gateway between mainland Asia and the islands of Japan, the Korea Peninsula has long been an attractive prize for other nations. At various times throughout history, the Korean people have lived under rule by China, Mongolia, Japan, and the Soviet Union. Even during these centuries of foreign control, however, Korea's population maintained a distinct cultural and political identity.

Scholars know little about the earliest inhabitants of the peninsula, although archaeologists have uncovered stone tools there estimated to be thirty thousand years old. Prehistoric Koreans are thought to have migrated to the peninsula from regions in modern Russia, Mongolia, and China, probably sometime around 4000 B.C.

● Ancient Chosun

According to popular legend, a leader named Dan-gun founded Korea in 2333 B.C. by uniting several ethnic groups into one kingdom. Dan-

gun is said to be the son of a heavenly prince and a bear that was transformed into a maiden. Called ancient Chosun, meaning "Land of the Morning Calm," Dan-gun's realm lasted more than one thousand years.

Centered in the Korea Peninsula's northwestern corner, Chosun eventually spread northward and westward beyond the peninsula. But in the twelfth century B.C., the Chinese state of Yan began to increase its power, eventually invading Chosun. Over time, ancient Chosun split into smaller units, and new states arose. Although the Chinese gradually lost their authority over most of the region, Chinese influence on the Korea Peninsula remained strong for centuries. In fact, Chinese ideas were important in shaping the region's civilization and government.

Around the first century B.C., several Korean groups united and formed the state of Koguryo in the northeastern part of the peninsula. Despite repeated attacks by the Chinese, Koguryo gained

In this sixth-century mural from North Korea, **Koguryo hunters** riding horses pursue big game with bows and arrows.

control of a portion of Manchuria (in modern China) and extended across the northern and central parts of the Korea Peninsula.

At the same time, other Korean states developed south of the Han River in modern South Korea. Baekje arose in the southwest in about A.D. 245, while the Silla kingdom emerged in the southeast. Meanwhile, to the north, Koguryo increased its strength. Each of these three major kingdoms would eventually adopt Buddhism, a religion that had been founded in India in the 500s B.C. and later adopted in China. The Chinese brought Buddhist scriptures to the Korea Peninsula in about A.D. 372, and the faith took hold in the region.

Koguryo expanded in the 500s and 600s, coming into conflict with the Sui dynasty of China to the west and with Silla to the south. Koguryo was able to repel the Sui forces. Silla leaders, however, allied themselves with the Chinese Tang dynasty. Silla's and Tang's combined forces overcame Baekje in 660 and went on to conquer Koguryo—which was plagued by famine and internal strife—in 668. The newly powerful Silla, like kingdoms before it, faced challenges from Chinese groups. But the unified Silla kingdom successfully resisted outside rule on most of the peninsula and developed an advanced society and culture.

Silla Dynasty

Silla power peaked in the mid-700s, when its rulers sought to create the ideal Buddhist state. Art, literature, and science thrived and developed during this period, and new policies distributed land more equally among peasants. In return, farmers gave rice, millet, barley, and wheat to the government.

Silla's capital city at Gyeongju (in modern South Korea) prospered. However, conflict arose as various wealthy families vied for powerful positions. Before long, Silla began to weaken from within, and by 900 it had split apart into three main kingdoms. These realms fought for control of the Korea Peninsula until 936, when they were unified by Wang Keon, the leader of one of the main regions.

The Koryo Kingdom

Under Wang Keon, the Korea Peninsula was ruled by a single kingdom again. Wang Keon named the region Koryo—from which the modern name "Korea" is derived—and extended the state's northern boundary to the Amnok. Along this northern river, Koryo forces frequently clashed with Manchurian troops from 993 to 1018. But Koryo held its position and established peace with Manchuria in 1022.

In the twelfth century, however, Koryo's stability began to crumble. Powerful families fought with the king for political control. Then, in 1170, military leaders rebelled, frustrated that they did not rank as highly as did other government officials. The soldiers seized power, and later kings served only as symbolic rulers with little authority.

Troubles worsened further in 1231, when Mongol warriors swept into Koryo from the north and overcame the kingdom. The powerful Mongol emperor Kublai Khan, hoping to conquer Japan also, enlisted Koreans in his expeditions. The Japanese repelled the Mongolian and Korean forces, but Koryo remained under the Mongols' domination.

After 1350 Japan and Koryo came into contact again, as Japanese pirates attacked the Korean coast with growing frequency. Yi Song-gye, a Koryo military commander, defeated the raiders in a series of battles. Along with this victory, he also gained influence in Koryo's politics.

In 1368 the Chinese Ming dynasty conquered the Mongols, who had also invaded Chinese territory. Many Koryo leaders were glad to be rid of the Mongols. But when the Ming took over Mongol holdings in Koryo, the kingdom simply faced another outside ruler. Koryo's king ordered General Yi Song-gye to attack Ming forces, but Yi thought that it would be wiser to forge friendly relations with the Ming. He revolted and turned his army against the capital. Yi seized the throne in 1392 and founded the Chosun dynasty.

Chosun Dynasty

During the Koryo dynasty, a group called the *yangban* had gained control of significant portions of farmland. The yangban were a class of scholar-officials, most of whom were highly educated in Confucian thought. Confucianism, like Buddhism, is a belief system that was introduced to Korea by the Chinese. Based on the ideas of the philosopher Confucius, it teaches a system of ethics and behavior based on strict class divisions, rank, and respect for authority.

Confucius

The yangban collected a high percentage of crops as rent from peasants who lived and worked on the land. The peasants also paid high taxes. During the Chosun dynasty, the yangban class grew rapidly and gained more and more land, putting still greater pressure on the peasants, who formed most of the population.

Buddhist monasteries also owned large amounts of land. But the monasteries lost both economic and political power when Chosun leaders abandoned Buddhism in favor of Confucianism as an ideal model for Korean life. As Buddhism declined, Korea became a primarily secular (nonreligious) society, since Confucianism is more of a philosophy than a religion.

King Sejong introduced many beneficial measures to his Chosun kingdom. For example, he passed tax reforms and health measures that greatly improved the lives of the people. Sejong also fostered the arts, science, and technology. In the 1440s, the king's strong support of education led to the invention of the Korean alphabet, named hangul (sometimes called "chosungul" in the North).

The greatest Chosun ruler was King Sejong, who reigned from 1418 to 1450. After Sejong's rule, however, Korea fell into the hands of less talented rulers. Succession to the throne often caused bitter struggles, and members of the yangban competed for power and desirable offices. Corruption became widespread as royal relatives and powerful factions increased their landholdings and wealth, while farmers faced ever-higher taxes and rents.

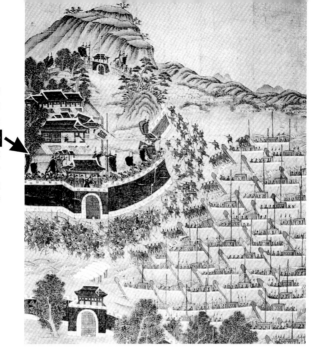

Korean soldiers defend the port of Busan in modern South Korea against an **attack by the Japanese** navy in the 1590s. Visit www.vgsbooks.com for links to more information about the rich history of the Korea Peninsula.

Foreign invasions only aggravated Korea's internal problems. Attacks by the Japanese in 1592 and 1597 and by Chinese forces in 1627 and 1636 upset the economy and ruined vast tracts of farmland. Koreans drove the Japanese off the peninsula, but the Chinese armies were too strong for them to defeat. Although the Chosun dynasty continued to rule, the state had to send tribute (payments) to the Chinese emperor.

Social and Economic Upheaval

During the seventeenth and eighteenth centuries, changing social and economic conditions brought about changes in Korean society. The economy grew, allowing a class of successful merchants to arise. As these merchants—some of them former peasants—became wealthier, the yangban's power declined, and common people were able to improve their social status more easily. Korean authors began to write of a society that valued equality and justice.

New schools of thought reflecting these social changes soon emerged. One was Sirhak, or "practical learning." Sirhak encompassed a respect for Korean history and culture, combined with a rejection of some of Confucianism's ideas in favor of Western science, technology, and social theory. This growing interest in Western thought influenced many Koreans. Although Chosun officials had closed their country to all foreigners except the Chinese, intending to protect Korean culture, China itself absorbed many European ideas about government, science, and philosophy. These ideas, in turn, came to Korea.

Western religion also had a growing impact. Roman Catholicism, brought to China by Portuguese missionaries, attracted followers among Koreans, who called it Seohak, or "Western learning." But while some Catholic beliefs—such as the equality of all people—appealed to

Koreans, they clashed with traditional Confucianism and ideas such as a rigid social order and ancestor worship. Chosun officials, hoping to preserve Confucian practices, soon outlawed Catholicism.

The economic and social developments that began in the 1600s and 1700s continued during the early 1800s. Ongoing struggles for power among rival officials thwarted political reform, but numerous peasant revolts did gradually lead to some improvements in farmers' lives. In addition, a leader named Choe Je-u formed a new movement called Donghak ("Eastern learning") in the mid-1800s. This blend of religion, philosophy, and politics combined elements of Asian beliefs, such as Confucianism and Buddhism, with modern ideas of social reform. The movement sought to end corruption and increase social justice within Korea.

International Involvement

Early in the nineteenth century, British ships arrived in Korean waters in an attempt to reach new Asian markets. By the 1840s, Russian and French merchants had also ventured into the region. Although the Korean government remained opposed to foreign contact, the Japanese became the first to break Korea's isolation in 1876, opening three Korean ports to Japanese trade. Meanwhile, China, feeling threatened by Japan's advances toward the peninsula, tried to reestablish its authority in the region.

Within Korea, opinion was divided. Some people wanted international contact, along with reform and modernization. Strong nationalist groups, on the other hand, sought independence from all foreign control. Fearing that nationalists threatened the Chosun dynasty's authority, the government quickly curbed their activities. But a new challenge to the dynasty arose in 1894, when followers of the Donghak movement gathered to protest the nation's corrupt and oppressive government. Peasant armies formed, and the protests soon spiraled into a full-scale revolt later known as the Donghak Rebellion. When the Chosun king asked Chinese troops to help quell the uprising, the Japanese—still seeking influence on the peninsula—sent in their own forces. The conflict erupted into the Sino-Japanese War, in which Japan defeated both China and the Donghak rebels.

According to the Treaty of Shimonoseki, which formally ended the war in 1895, Chinese influence over Korea was lessened. However, the Japanese, instead, became increasingly involved in Korean affairs. They encouraged social and political reforms to prevent further internal problems in Korea.

While Japan was extending its control in eastern Asia, Russia had also increased its presence in the region. In addition to taking over parts of northeastern China, Russia tried to claim a share of Korea's forests and mines. Resulting rivalry between Russia and Japan erupted in the Russo-Japanese War in 1904. Japan won the war, this time deciding to tighten its hold over the much sought-after peninsula. In 1905 Korea became a Japanese protectorate (dependent state), and on August 22, 1910, Japan claimed Korea as a colony.

Under Japan

The Japanese colonial government enacted many changes. Koreans were treated as a conquered and inferior people, and their culture was destroyed or covered up. For example, Pyongyang's name was changed to Heijo, and many buildings were torn down and replaced with new Japanese structures. The colonizers prevented Koreans from publishing their own newspapers and from organizing political or intellectual groups. Japanese officials also tightened control over Korean education and shut down private schools. Many Koreans lost their land, and thousands were arrested on suspicions of working against the Japanese. Many were tortured or killed.

The Japanese forced **Korea's last king, Kojong,** to abdicate (leave office) in 1907. Three years later, they abolished the Chosun dynasty, which had ruled Korea since 1392.

FIGHTING FOR FREEDOM

"We herewith proclaim the independence of Korea and the liberty of the Korean people. We tell it to the world in witness of the equality of all nations and we pass it on to our posterity as their inherent right.... We take this step to insure to our children for all time to come, personal liberty in accord with the awakening consciousness of this new era. This is the clear leading of God, the moving principle of the present age, the whole human race's just claim. It is something that cannot be stamped out, or stifled, or gagged, or suppressed by any means."

—from the March First "Proclamation of Korean Independence," 1919

In 1919, rebelling against such brutal treatment, Korean nationalists seeking Korean independence organized a protest known as the March First Movement. The demonstration, which quickly expanded into a nationwide uprising, was harshly put down by Japanese forces and failed to achieve its goals. However, it did mark a push for freedom, democracy, and national identity that unified all Koreans, regardless of social class. Over the next two decades, Korean resistance to Japanese rule grew stronger and more organized. In turn, Japanese colonial officials increased repression, and efforts to erase Korean culture continued. Colonial rulers instructed Koreans to replace their loyalty to Korea with allegiance to Japan. A law required Koreans to worship at Shinto shrines (monuments to the traditional Japanese religion), and Japanese officials forced Koreans to adopt Japanese names. Teachers began to use the Japanese language and to instruct students in Japanese history and culture. Speaking Korean was forbidden.

◉ Communist Beginnings

Under Japan's oppressive rule, some Korean students and workers began seeking political alternatives. Inspired by a Communist revolution in Russia in 1917 and similar movements in China, they began forming Korean Communist parties in the 1920s.

By the 1930s, Korean Communists had begun launching guerrilla-style attacks against the Japanese. The guerrillas worked in small, mobile units, carrying out ambushes, sabotage, and other unconventional warfare. Korean groups had headquarters in China, the Soviet Union, or Manchuria, which, like Korea, had been occupied by the Japanese. Chinese and Soviet Communists frequently worked alongside the Koreans in their fight. Around this time, a young man from northern Korea named Kim Song-ju, who later took the name

Kim Il Sung was twenty-nine years old when World War II came to eastern Asia. He was already a respected leader.

Kim Il Sung, emerged as a prominent guerrilla fighter and Communist leader.

Meanwhile, Japan's military power and its hunger for new territory grew. Korea became the base for Japan's planned invasion of China, and Korean youths were drafted into the Japanese army. In preparation for the expected war, Japan increased farming within Korea to meet the Japanese demand for more rice. Large-scale industry also grew. Economic growth, however, benefited the Japanese who controlled Korea, not the Koreans themselves. By the 1930s, half of Korea's rice was going to Japan, while many Koreans starved. When World War II reached eastern Asia in 1941, conditions worsened further. Koreans experienced even more drastic food shortages, and Japanese oppression increased.

Division

In 1945 World War II ended with Japan's defeat. The Soviet Union and the United States—which had both been on the winning Allied side—agreed to divide the Korea Peninsula at roughly the 38th Parallel of latitude and to share the work of getting the newly independent country back on its feet. Intending their stay to be brief, Soviet troops occupied northern Korea and U.S. troops were stationed in the South.

Koreans were grateful to be free of Japanese rule, but new challenges soon developed. During the next two years, the Soviet and U.S. powers worked toward unifying the peninsula—a goal shared by Koreans on both sides of the temporary dividing line. Conferences between the United States and the Soviet Union, however, deteriorated into mistrust as these two nations' interests conflicted in other parts of the world.

Moving ahead independently, leaders in the northern peninsula began organizing a government. In early 1946, the Provisional People's Committee was founded in Pyongyang. The group was headed by Kim Il Sung, who had remained an important figure in the Communist movement and whom Soviet officials had chosen as a promising leader. The Soviet Union handed over control to the new committee, which began directing the establishment of a Communist system. Soon thereafter the Korean Workers' Party (KWP) was formed, uniting several Communist groups into one official ruling party under Kim's leadership. Meanwhile, the U.S.-aided southern region established a democratic government.

In 1947, still hoping to see one Korea, the United States submitted the unification problem to the United Nations (UN), a new organization formed to handle international disputes. The UN offered to supervise a single set of elections for the country, but northern officials refused to allow UN representatives into the North. On September 9, 1948, northern leaders announced the formation of the Democratic People's Republic of Korea, with Kim Il Sung as its head and effective dictator.

In the South, similar changes were in progress. The Republic of Korea was founded with Syngman Rhee as its elected president. Both the northern and southern governments claimed to represent all of the Korea Peninsula, and for the time being, reunification was on hold.

COLD SNAP

Soon after World War II, a political conflict known as the Cold War began. Named because it never erupted into a "hot," or military war, the conflict pitted Communist nations, such as the Soviet Union, against anti-Communist nations, such as the United States. Each nation tried to gain influence and to prevent the opposite side from expanding in territory or power. With the Soviet Union and the United States attempting to share the Korea Peninsula, the Cold War was one of the main forces behind the ongoing division.

◎ The Korean War

Between 1948 and 1950, North and South Korean troops clashed along the 38th Parallel several times. Meanwhile, North Korea amassed the large Korean People's Army, which had grown out of the Soviet-supported guerrilla groups in which Kim Il Sung and other Koreans had fought against Japanese occupation.

Despite ongoing tensions, the United States and the Soviet Union withdrew their troops in 1948 and 1949. But the lingering tension soon exploded into war. With U.S. defense forces gone, DPRK leaders saw an opportunity to reunify the peninsula by force. On June 25, 1950, North Korean troops invaded South Korea.

Thousands of North Korean troops poured across the 38th Parallel. Many soldiers went into battle believing northern propaganda (ideas spread to enforce a desired mindset) claiming that the United States had attacked Korea and that North Korea was acting out of self-defense. In fact, the United States and other members of the UN sent military forces to South Korea within a few days of the invasion. However, the North Korean army quickly captured the peninsula as far as the Busan Perimeter, a curving line of defense to the north and east of the South Korean city of Busan.

On September 15, U.S. soldiers launched a surprise attack, landing at Incheon on the northwestern coast of South Korea. Their arrival was paired with an aggressive aerial campaign that blanketed the North with bombs and napalm (a sticky, gasoline-based substance that burns on contact). This attack turned the tide of the war. U.S., UN, and South Korean troops, seeing their own chance to reunify Korea, pushed northward and neared the Amnok by October 1950. But

U.S. B-29 Superfortresses fly a bombing mission over North Korea in 1950.

Many historians have discussed why China entered the Korean War, and many theories exist. Some say that China—which at that time was the world's second-largest Communist nation after the Soviet Union—wanted all of Korea to become Communist. Others suggest that Chinese leaders feared that the anti-Communist United States would invade their nation next. China may also have been repaying a favor, as many North Koreans fought in China's 1949 Communist Revolution.

that same month, China sent troops of its own across the border to defend North Korea. The southern army was driven back, arriving south of Seoul, South Korea's capital, in early 1951.

Truce talks began in July 1951, but fighting continued for two more years. The opposing forces settled on a cease-fire in 1953, but a permanent peace treaty was never signed. A 2.4-mile-wide (3.9-km) buffer area called the Demilitarized Zone was established, dividing the two sides. After more than three years of war, only about 1,500 square miles (3, 885 sq. km) of territory changed hands, moving from North Korean to South Korean control. Meanwhile, U.S. forces remained stationed at South Korean bases.

Koreans paid a heavy toll in human lives and in property damage, resulting in an estimated 1.5 million North Koreans dead and wounded, plus millions of dollars of damage. The war also left deep emotional scars on the Korean people, who began to realize that the division of their homeland would last much longer than they had imagined. In the years following the war, leaders from the North and South made occasional attempts to discuss reunification. Tensions and mistrust still ran high on both sides of the DMZ, and in North Korea, hostility against the United States was especially strong.

◉ Rebuilding

While preparing for World War II, the Japanese had concentrated their industries in the North. Although the Korean War had destroyed many facilities, the basic groundwork for industrial production remained. In 1954 the KWP launched a "Three-Year Plan" to get the nation's economy on track, and industrial development began at a rapid pace. Factory workers were organized into production teams and were driven to work hard for the benefit of the young republic.

Other major changes included land reform. Collectivization began, pooling farmland to be shared and farmed cooperatively by teams of

On this **collective farm** near Anju-up in northwestern North Korea, workers' houses with traditional tiled roofs look out over the collective's dusty fields.

peasants. However, ownership of homes and gardens was still private, and many people grew vegetables or raised a few animals to help feed their families and to sell at markets for extra income.

These new programs dramatically increased industrial and agricultural output in the 1950s. Large numbers of North Koreans saw improvement in their standard of living, a welcome change after the hardships of Japanese control and two wars. To many, it appeared that Kim's government was, indeed, putting the nation back on track.

Kim's Korea

Throughout the mid-1950s and early 1960s, Kim began adapting classic Soviet theories of Communism to fit his own vision of North Korea and its place in the world and to incorporate some of Confucianism's principles. The most important idea to come from this process was *juche.* This concept centered on self-reliance, strongly stressing the need for North Korea to be independent of other nations and to refuse outside help and influence—a policy that recalled Korea's historical Hermit Kingdom days.

Building on the juche idea as well as on Communism, the government also promoted a movement centered on three main areas of development: ideological, technical, and cultural. This movement, which eventually became known as the Three Revolutions, was a guiding force in the nation's progress. KWP officials urged the population to embrace juche ideology, to advance North Korea's technical capabilities, and to protect national culture.

Over time, Kim's increasingly strict idea of how juche and other policies should be followed led to conflicts within the government. These internal disagreements periodically resulted in purges, in which dissenting officials were fired, imprisoned, or even tortured or executed for treason. Meanwhile, Kim was presented to the population as their Great Leader, who was kind, wise, and without faults. This cult of personality was reinforced by propaganda distributed by the KWP and through the nation's state-run media. That same propaganda declared that other nations—especially the anti-Communist United States, which was singled out for its role in the Korean War and for its capitalist system—were inferior to North Korea and should be regarded as enemies.

Mounting Challenges

Although North Korea's system initially spurred economic growth and other improvements, by the mid-1970s, the country faced shortages of food and fuel—due in part to its strict juche policy of refusing outside trade. As conditions began to worsen, officials sought to control unrest. Punishment of citizens who criticized or disobeyed Kim or his government grew more common and more severe. During the 1970s, thousands of North Koreans were labeled "counterrevolutionaries" and were sent—usually with their whole families—to forced labor camps located in remote regions. Prisoners of these camps faced harsh living conditions, backbreaking work, and often death.

This 70-foot (23-m) **statue of Kim Il Sung,** which stands on a hill in Pyongyang, was completed for his sixtieth birthday in 1972. Find links to more information about modern North Korea by going to www.vgsbooks.com.

For the government, a new challenge arose in the 1980s with the question of who would eventually succeed Kim Il Sung as the nation's leader. Many expected Kim's younger brother, Kim Yong Ju, to fill that role. However, it soon became clear that Kim Il Sung hoped to place his son Kim Jong-il in power. The issue became increasingly problematic as opponents of Kim Jong-il—whom many believed was incompetent—grew more vocal. At the same time, troubles multiplied as worker uprisings, fed by dissatisfaction with pay and working conditions, erupted in cities throughout the country between 1981 and 1983. But government forces put down these protests harshly, killing hundreds, and the KWP and Kim Il Sung maintained their grip on power.

A Nuclear Nation?

Ever since division and the Korean War, North-South relations had been strained. Although both sides hoped for eventual reunification and several talks had taken place to discuss the issue, progress remained elusive and efforts had dwindled. Attempts to improve inter-Korean relations were finally revived in the late 1980s, when South Korean president Roh Tae-woo proposed ideas for trade, family visits, and other cooperation between the two Koreas. A series of diplomatic talks between northern and southern officials resulted between 1989 and 1992.

However, international attention soon turned from reunification to a growing nuclear crisis. North Korea, as a member of the Nuclear Non-Proliferation Treaty, or NPT (an international agreement to control, dismantle, and prevent development of nuclear weapons), allowed International Atomic Energy Association (IAEA) inspectors to view certain sites within the country in 1992. These sites included nuclear energy plants, but North Korea later refused to permit further inspection of other areas, such as military facilities. Global suspicions skyrocketed, and U.S. officials accused the North of hiding illegal weapons programs.

UNDERGROUND WAR

Even as some attempts were made to foster positive relations between North and South Korea, hostile exchanges also occurred over the years. For example, the South had planned secret attacks on the North that included a failed assassination plot against Kim Il Sung in the late 1960s. The North had tried to assassinate South Korean president Park Chung-hee in 1968, and North Korean terrorists killed seven South Korean officials on a government visit to Burma in 1983. In addition, North Korean agents kidnapped South Korean citizens (as well as Japanese) in the 1970s and 1980s, possibly to provide the North's spies with information.

BUILDING BOMBS?

North Korea has large reserves of the radioactive element uranium, and it used this resource to power its first nuclear energy plants. A by-product of such plants is plutonium, another radioactive substance, which is used in nuclear bombs. However, relatively large amounts of plutonium, along with advanced technology, are needed to create nuclear weapons. It remains unknown whether North Korea has these resources or not, but many outside observers believe that North Korea either has nuclear weapons already or is working to produce them. The North's leadership itself sometimes claims to have weapons and other times denies the charge—apparently preferring to keep the details uncertain for strategic reasons.

The United States also announced that it would conduct Team Spirit "war games" in South Korea, a large-scale training exercise simulating nuclear war on the peninsula. Responding both to the accusations and to the war games, which it saw as a threat, North Korea announced that it was pulling out of the NPT in March 1993.

In the midst of this crisis, North Korea was thrown into deeper turmoil by the death of Kim Il Sung on July 8, 1994. Although Kim J ong-il was still expected to be his father's successor, he did not immediately assume leadership. Said to be observing a traditional three-year period of mourning, Kim Jong-il made few public appearances in the following months, and it seemed to many North Koreans that no clear leader was in charge at all. (Kim Jong-il would not officially become head of the KWP and, therefore, of the nation until 1997.) Internal troubles deepened when severe floods struck between 1994 and 1996, followed by devastating famine. As millions starved and thousands defected to South Korea and other nations to escape the hunger, North Korea—unable to cope with the situation alone—broke from past practices and requested outside aid.

Meanwhile, a series of intense negotiations had followed the initial nuclear scare. Over the course of the mid- to late 1990s, a variety of proposals were suggested. Among other things, the United States agreed to support financial aid to North Korea, to discuss reducing U.S. military presence in South Korea, and to help the North develop and modernize its nuclear energy facilities. In return, North Korea stayed in the NPT and ended any nuclear weapons programs, missile testing, and similar activities. However, relations continued to be strained between North Korea and the United States, and although the crisis gradually waned, no decisive agreement had been put into motion by the turn of the century.

During **the 2000 summit meeting,** South Korean president Kim Dae-jung *(left)* and North Korea's leader Kim Jong-il *(right)* discussed many issues of mutual concern. However, in 2002 the South Korean government and the South's large Hyundai Corporation were accused of bribing Kim Jong-il to agree to the summit, by paying the North more than $1 billion.

Gradual Opening and Ongoing Struggles

In June 2000, Kim Jong-il and South Korean president Kim Dae-jung met at a summit in Pyongyang. The occasion marked the first time North Korea had welcomed a president from the South, and images of the two leaders shaking hands were broadcast around the globe. Meanwhile, the North Korean government had begun to explore new economic directions and had also allowed several nations to open embassies in Pyongyang. Many hoped that these developments signified a further opening of the "hermit" state and a new era of international cooperation.

But soon thereafter, the nuclear issue returned to the forefront. North Korean officials, claiming frustration with the lack of progress in setting up planned U.S.-aided nuclear power plants, threatened to resume weapons development. The situation deteriorated further in early 2002. U.S. president George W. Bush grouped the nation with Iraq and Iran in a so-called "axis of evil" because of its nuclear weapons program, and international focus on the nation intensified. North Korea responded by removing cameras from its nuclear sites, refusing inspections, claiming to have continued secret development, and withdrawing from the NPT. Talks between North and South Korea in January 2003 failed to defuse the crisis, and tensions heightened as the U.S. and North Korean governments hurled insults at each other. Some U.S. officials hinted that military force could be used if necessary and once again announced its intention to hold war games in the South. Meanwhile, North Korea hinted at threats of its own by testing several nonnuclear missiles. New talks began in February 2004, this time bringing in representatives from North and South Korea, the United States, Russia, China, and Japan.

In April 2004, attentions shifted once more when a train accident caused a massive explosion that rocked Ryongchon, a town in northeastern North Korea, ten miles southeast of the Chinese border. The North Korean government was secretive about the exact causes of the accident, as well as about the death toll. However, it did make the somewhat unusual move of asking international aid agencies for help, and workers who were allowed into the country reported that hundreds had been injured and that thousands of homes had been flattened or damaged by the blast. As this immediate crisis took center stage, the nuclear question moved to the background for the time being.

A more positive development was a breakthrough in inter-Korean relations that took place in June, as North-South talks led to an agreement to reduce propaganda along the edges of the DMZ. Propaganda measures had included loudspeakers broadcasting music and messages from the North, and electronic billboards displaying news and other information from the South. That same month, both North and South Korea welcomed the announcement that the United States planned to pull more than 12,000 of its troops out of South Korea. The figure represents about one-third of

In the aftermath of the **2004 Ryongchon accident,** the North Korean press praised people whom it claimed had died while rushing into buildings to save portraits of Kim Il Sung and Kim Jong-il from destruction.

the total number of troops stationed on the peninsula, most of them along the DMZ.

A different kind of news was reported in July 2004, when South Korea accepted more than four hundred North Korean defectors into the country. The unusually large group, made up of people who had been in hiding in Vietnam after escaping the North, highlighted the rising number of defectors since the early 2000s. While officials in the South stated that the new arrivals were refugees seeking asylum, North Korean officials condemned the act, claiming that its citizens had been kidnapped. Many outside observers watched the situation carefully, hoping that the incident would not threaten future talks between the Koreas or hinder the resolution of the nuclear issue.

Government

The Democratic People's Republic of Korea's 1998 constitution designates Kim Il Sung as Eternal President of the nation. As a result, his successor and son, Kim Jong-il, does not hold the title of president. However, Kim Jong-il rules as a dictator and is the highest authority in the nation, with titles including Chairman of the National Defense Commission and General Secretary of the Korean Workers' Party. He is also known as the Dear Leader.

A body called the Supreme People's Assembly (SPA) forms the government's legislative branch. Members hold four-year terms, and while all North Koreans seventeen years of age and older may vote for SPA officials, the elections appear to be held only for show. Voter turnout is usually reported as close to 100 percent, with 100 percent of the votes cast for candidates that have been chosen by the KWP. Most upper-lever officials are men, although some women do rise through party ranks to prominent positions.

Two executive bodies called the Central People's Committee and the State Administration Council also play roles in the country's management. Members of these groups are chosen by the SPA, Kim Jong-il, and his advisers. The Central Court heads North Korea's judicial branch, with judges elected to four-year terms by the Supreme People's Assembly.

Below the federal level, Local People's Committees and Local Administrative Committees handle regional matters. Their members are elected, but, again, the elections are not believed to be truly democratic, and these committees are made up of party members chosen by the KWP and upper-level officials.

Similarly, the KWP has small local committees nationwide. Headed by the Party Congress, the KWP is the country's most important political party. In fact, while other parties technically exist, the KWP is the only one with any real power, and many North Koreans are members.

THE PEOPLE

With a population of about 22.7 million people, North Korea's average population density is 487 people per square mile (188 per sq. km), compared to 1,251 people per square mile (483 people per sq. km) in neighboring South Korea and to 70 people per square mile (30 per sq. km) in the United States. Because so much of North Korea is mountainous, however, the true population density in Pyongyang and other cities is actually considerably higher. About 60 percent of the nation's people live in these urban areas.

The vast majority of the nation's population is ethnically Korean, as very few foreigners live in North Korea. In fact, the nation prides itself on its uniformity of heritage. But while North Koreans share a common language, culture, and background, their exact origins as a people are uncertain. Korean legend holds that Dan-gun was the founder of both the Korean nation and its people in 2333 B.C., while most scholars believe that Koreans descended from nomadic peoples from Mongolia much earlier. In any case, despite periods of outside

rule over the centuries, the ethnic makeup of peoples living on the Korea Peninsula remained largely unchanged.

Nevertheless, Korea did not remain entirely untouched. Throughout its long history as a link between Chinese and Japanese cultures, the nation absorbed and adapted ideas from both of these neighbors, and many traits of the Korean people were shaped by these outside influences. Western ideas arrived in the 1600s, and after the end of World War II, North Korea was also strongly affected by the Soviet Union.

Modern North Korea has, once again, largely closed itself off to most of the outside world. The government carefully monitors information and other materials entering, exiting, and within the country—returning the nation, in many ways, to Korea's days as the Hermit Kingdom. But as in the past, these measures do not isolate the nation completely, and North Korea's contact with the larger world gradually continues to expand.

◉ Social Structure

The three most common Korean surnames (last names) are Kim, Lee (sometimes Yi or Rhee), and Park (sometimes romanized as Pak). In Korean culture, the surname appears before the given name. In addition, the given name usually has two syllables. For example, Kim Jong-il has the surname Kim and the personal name Jong-il.

When Western influence first reached Korea in the 1600s, the nation had a rigid social structure defined primarily by Confucianism. Within this framework, individuals and social groups were defined by their status relative to each other. For example, members of the small upper classes—which included scholars and government officials—were considered superior to lower classes, whose much larger numbers included small-scale farmers, merchants, craftspeople, and slaves. Lower classes were expected to respect and obey the higher classes.

These social conventions extended to the family, which formed the most basic and important element in the Korean social organization. In some cases, particularly among the wealthy, households included extended family such as grandparents, aunts, uncles, and cousins. Family largely determined an individual's place in society. The family, therefore, was more highly valued than the individual.

Also in keeping with Confucian guidelines, status within the family and social classes was based primarily on age and gender. Korean children and youths were always expected to respect and honor their elders. Women held the lowest positions, were responsible for almost all of the parenting duties, and very rarely worked outside the home.

The establishment of a Communist government in the late 1940s changed many of these norms. In theory, under the leadership of the Korean Workers' Party, all citizens are considered equal, regardless of wealth, gender, age, or education. In addition, all are required to work if they are able—male or female. As a result, most North Korean women hold jobs, and many are in the military—both of which mark a departure from historical and traditional standards.

Nevertheless, some discrimination does exist in practice. A small number of high-ranking members of the KWP are favored with finer homes, cars, and greater access to food supplies, while average North Koreans have fewer of these privileges.

Along with party loyalty, family ties are still among the most important in the society, and respect for parents and other elders remains strong. This ancient Korean value is, in part, reflected by

This **young family in Kaesung** is on the move. Family ties remain strong in North Korea.

widespread propaganda that encourages a deep reverence for the ruling Kim family. Family is also very important when it comes to marriage. Some matches in North Korea are set up by parents, other relatives, or professional matchmakers, with the bride and groom never having met in some cases. Among couples who choose their partners themselves, an obstacle that sometimes arises is a remaining social stigma against families whose members worked with or for the Japanese during the colonial period. Anyone who is seen as having cooperated with the Japanese occupation in any way is considered inferior, and parents—or sometimes KWP officials—often forbid their sons and daughters from marrying relatives of these people.

Housing and Health

Traditional Korean homes were one-story structures made of brick or concrete blocks and roofed with tiles, slate, or zinc. A typical house had a living room, a kitchen, and a bedroom. However, after the destruction of World War II and the Korean War, many Koreans were homeless or lived in crowded, run-down homes without running water or other basics.

KEEPING COZY

Since as long ago as 300 B.C., a heating system called *ondol* has warmed Korean homes. In this system, stone pipes under the floor carried hot air from the kitchen fire. The ondol system is still used in modern homes and may be heated by electricity, natural gas, steam, or coal. The warmest spot on the floor is traditionally given to guests.

The new Communist government soon set about rebuilding the country, and land reform helped to improve the quality of life for many North Koreans in the 1950s. Rural life was, in many ways, much as it had been for centuries, with most families inhabiting small, modest homes. These countryside dwellings remain the best examples of traditional architecture in North Korea, because in Pyongyang most older structures were destroyed and many have been replaced. Newer housing in the capital includes a number of massive high-rise apartment buildings that were erected in the 1980s.

After the destructive war years, during which millions of North Koreans were killed or injured, the early years of the DPRK saw a relative improvement in the population's health. The Communist government provided food and medical care for all citizens, and living conditions rose. But economic setbacks in the 1980s and 1990s crippled the health system and left much of the population without access to doctors, hospitals, or medication. Increasingly frequent power outages often cut off heat, running water, and other necessities.

Then, following severe floods that devastated crop yields in the mid-1990s, a devastating famine struck the nation. This drastic food shortage was the single largest factor affecting the health of most North Koreans in the late twentieth and early twenty-first centuries, killing huge numbers of people between 1995 and 1999. Estimates range widely, pegging the number of deaths anywhere between 200,000 and 3 million. Although the nation requested outside aid, accepting shipments of food and allowing some international

In Kaesung, **modern high-rise apartment buildings** contrast with a passing ox-drawn cart. Particularly outside of Pyongyang, few North Koreans own motor vehicles. Traditional means of transportation persist. To read more about everyday life in North Korea, go to www.vgsbooks.com for links.

Through the **UN's World Food Programme,** these workers in the North Korean city of Chongjin receive daily food supplies for their labor. Their goal is to deepen a riverbed in the hopes of preventing future floods.

organizations to enter the country, the crisis proved difficult to stem. While the famine has eased, thousands of North Koreans are still believed to be living in hunger. A lack of adequate nutrition also places people at higher risk for disease, and tuberculosis is thought to be a growing problem in North Korea.

Children and the elderly are especially vulnerable to these health dangers, and North Korean statistics show the results. For example, the number of North Korean infants who die in the first year of life was estimated at 45 out of every 1,000—considerably higher than the East Asian average of 29. Similarly, the average North Korean's estimated life expectancy stands at 63 years, compared to 76 in South Korea. These figures reflect, in part, high levels of malnutrition and related health problems.

Other serious health risks include acquired immune deficiency syndrome (AIDS), a deadly disease caused by human immunodeficiency virus (HIV), as well as severe acute respiratory syndrome (SARS), an illness that has periodically swept Asia since the early 2000s. While these are global concerns, North Korea has released little information on their impact within the country, so it is unknown how many residents might suffer from one of them. However, the limited traffic between North Korea and other nations could potentially protect the population from widespread exposure to such epidemics.

Human Rights

Internationally, one of the gravest concerns regarding the North Korean people is the status of their human rights. Although the nation's constitution technically guarantees citizens certain civil rights, the government greatly limits these liberties in practice, and many outside observers believe that North Koreans' human rights are regularly and seriously violated.

The worst violations take place in the nation's labor camps. Also called concentration camps, or gulags, these sites are estimated to hold up to 200,000 people. Many of these prisoners are arrested by the People's Security Force, the DPRK's main internal security arm. North Koreans can be sent to the camps for committing a variety of crimes that are often vaguely defined or for violating laws that they may not be aware exist. Usually such crimes are related to criticism of or defiance against the government. Entire families may be arrested and sent to camps because of the actions of one member, or families may be split apart and spouses forced to divorce. Inmates of the camps are believed to be severely underfed, harshly treated, and forced to do hard labor, and many are probably tortured or executed.

In addition, charges emerged in early 2004 that the North Korean government was testing gas, poison,

---

A NORTH KOREAN VOICE

"I don't want to see any more skeletal children with wide, frightened eyes. I don't want any more children sent to the camps and their mothers forced to divorce their fathers. I want their grandfathers to be around to tell them stories—and their giggles on the banks of the Daedong never to be interrupted by the arrival of bureaucrats from the Security Force."

—from *Aquariums of Pyongyang* by Kang Chol-Hwan, who spent ten years in a North Korean camp and has gone on to work for human rights and other chemical weapons on camp inmates. Although these claims have not been proven, many survivors, defectors, and outside observers believe that they are plausible, given the verifiable information that is available about the camps. Others have charged that pregnant prisoners are regularly forced to have abortions or, if they give birth, to put their infants to death. This practice is believed to be especially common when women who have fled to China are caught and returned to North Korea, as the DPRK is said to want Korean ethnicity to remain unmixed.

Less life-threatening but broader, day-to-day restrictions of human rights include surveillance of citizens' movements, telephone conversations, letters, and other activities; the strict control of travel within the country; the suppression of religious worship; and the restriction of freedoms of speech, press, and assembly. In addition, though famine continues to grip the country, most high-ranking officials are believed to have adequate food, and significant funds are still spent for nonessential military and government purposes such as celebrations.

Education

Education has a long history in Korea, dating back to the Dae-hak. This "great school," or university, was founded in the state of Koguryo in the northeastern part of the Korea Peninsula in A.D. 372. However, until the late 1800s, only the sons of the yangban attended school. That changed at the end of the nineteenth century, when Christian missionaries opened schools that offered education to more Koreans, including women.

Under Japanese rule between 1910 and 1945, the school system changed again. Instructors began teaching Japanese culture, as well as offering technical courses that prepared Koreans to work in an industrialized society. At the same time, the Japanese severely limited educational opportunities in other ways. They closed private schools, strictly controlled the curriculum, and conducted all classes in Japanese. Many Koreans remained illiterate during this period.

After World War II and the Korean War, rebuilding and modernizing schools was one of the challenges facing North Korea. Only about 30 percent of children were attending any school, and most people could not read or write. Using the Soviet Union's school system as an example, the DPRK government tackled these problems by making education free and compulsory. Schools resumed teaching in the Korean language, and the nation's literacy rate rose quickly, reaching an estimated 95 to 99 percent by the early 2000s.

All modern North Korean children are required to attend eleven years of school, which are free of charge. One year of preschool begins

North Korean students, such as these gathered for a Korean Workers' Party (KWP) celebration in Nampo, study Kim Il Sung's life, his juche idea, and his ideas about Communism. Kim Jong-il's biography and writings are also taught. However, the history taught in North Korean schools—on both their country and its leaders—is believed to be distorted and peppered with propaganda.

at about age five, followed by four years of primary school and six of secondary. The top North Korean students follow this schooling with time at colleges or universities, which are also free. The most respected upper-level institution is Kim Il Sung University in Pyongyang.

Language

Korean began as a distinct language, and for the most part, it has remained separate from the languages of its neighbors China and Japan. Most experts group it with other languages that originated in the Altay Mountains of central Asia. This category also includes the Mongolian, Turkish, and Finnish languages.

However, the Korean language has changed over time. When the hangul alphabet was created in the 1440s, it largely replaced the Chinese characters that had been used up until that time. Consisting of ten vowels and fourteen consonants, which are arranged in syllables rather than in words, the alphabet is considered to be one of the most logical writing systems in the world. It made reading and writing easier for all Koreans, and literacy increased dramatically after its introduction.

In addition, Korean borrowed words from Chinese over the course of many years, until as much as half of Korean's vocabulary was more closely related to Chinese than to Korean. However, after division and the formation of the DPRK, the North Korean government officially prohibited the use of foreign words. However, South Koreans continued to borrow some vocabulary from the outside. At the same time, despite the North's effort to keep the language isolated, North Koreans are influenced by the languages of their Russian and Chinese neighbors, while South Koreans have more contact with Japanese and English. The result of all of these factors is that Koreans from the North and the South find it harder and harder to understand one another—a development that may complicate any future reunification.

FAMILY REUNIONS

Of all the changes that resulted from the Korea Peninsula's division—from unexpected language barriers to different versions of history—the most painful was the division of families. Millions of North Koreans were separated from relatives in the South, and citizens of the two nations were not allowed to see each other. However, beginning in 2000, the governments of the two Koreas have begun arranging visits between family members. These highly emotional reunions bring together parents, children, siblings, spouses, and other family members who have not seen each other—or often, even communicated—in fifty years.

A North Korean husband *(right)* embraces his South Korean wife and daughter during a North-South exchange. Tens of thousands of Koreans on both sides apply. Only one hundred from each side are accepted for each exchange.

CULTURAL LIFE

North Korea's uniquely complex past—as both a long-isolated realm and a historical bridge among cultures and eras—has given it a unique and rich cultural heritage. While the Communist government has largely suppressed some forms of cultural expression, it has also placed a high value on traditional arts, which live on in the modern DPRK.

Religion

Most Communist governments, including North Korea, discourage or ban the practice of religion. In North Korea, reverence for juche and the personality cult surrounding the Kim family have, in some ways, become the state religion. And while the North Korean constitution technically allows limited religious activity, it is largely forbidden in practice.

Nevertheless, many North Koreans are believed to follow their faiths in secret, drawing on a long and rich history of religion on the Korea Peninsula. Shamanism, Buddhism, Confucianism, and Christianity

have all influenced Korea over the centuries, and each has left its mark.

Shamanism is the oldest belief system on the Korea Peninsula. Early Korean shamanists believed that the universe and everything in it are sacred and that each part of nature—from the sun and moon to rocks and trees—contains a spirit. Buddhism and Confucianism came to Korea later, arriving from China between the fourth and seventh centuries A.D. Buddhism was founded in India in the sixth century B.C., by Siddhartha Gautama (Buddha). Buddhism's ideas of reaching peace and happiness through a simple life of virtue and wisdom strongly influenced Koreans until almost the fifteenth century. Then, during the Chosun dynasty (1392–1910), Confucianism replaced Buddhism as the state belief system. Founded by the Chinese philosopher Confucius in the 500s B.C., Confucianism is based on a set of ethical concepts to guide behavior and does not teach the existence of divine beings.

Christianity first entered Korea in the 1600s, when Confucian scholars began studying the religion and bringing its ideas from China to Korea. Further influence arrived with Catholic missionaries in 1785 and with Protestants in the 1880s. Christian missionary work—despite resistance and persecution by the government—was especially successful in northern Korea, and dozens of Christian churches were built in Pyongyang during the late 1800s.

A new faith called Cheondogyo, or "Religion of the Heavenly Way," also emerged in the 1800s. Cheondogyo combined ideas from other religions in Korea, bringing together elements of Confucianism, Buddhism, and Christianity in one belief system.

In modern North Korea, all of these beliefs are believed to have underground followings. However, citizens who are caught practicing their faiths may be severely punished.

◎ Holidays and Festivals

Because of governmental restrictions, religious holidays are not a major part of North Korean life. Although a few traditional festivals are observed, including the lunar new year and Chuseok (the autumn Harvest Moon Festival), the most important special occasions tend to glorify events in the DPRK's history. Perhaps the largest festivities are reserved for the birthday of Kim Il Sung, on April 15, and the two-day celebration of Kim Jong-il's birthday held on February 16 and 17.

Parades, concerts, artistic performances, and fireworks all mark these events. The study of Kim Il Sung's and Kim Jong-il's writings is encouraged, and poems and other compositions praising the government and the father and son are read aloud at public gatherings.

In 1997 North Korea adopted the new "juche calendar," which uses 1912, the year of Kim Il Sung's birth, as year 1. Therefore, the year 2004 was Juche 93.

May Day is another popular holiday, and a major celebration is usually held on May 1 at Pyongyang's large May Day Stadium. A highlight of the event is the sight of hundreds of costumed children performing rhythmic gymnastics in perfect unison, creating colorful, complex shapes and patterns on the field. On this and other special occasions, North Korean stadium audiences are also known for their elaborate card displays. In these performances, people seated in the stands hold up colored cards in prearranged patterns to spell out words or to create images.

A number of other holidays are also observed in North Korea throughout the year. These include New Year's Day (January 1), International Women's Day (March 8), Liberation Day (August 15, marking Japan's

featuring Kim Il Sung *(upper right)* is the backdrop for an exhibition of rhythmic gymnastics.

surrender at the end of World War II in 1945), and the anniversary of the KWP's founding (October 10).

⊙ Food and Dress

Although the Korea Peninsula has a long culinary tradition, with a cuisine famous for its spiciness and rich flavors, most modern North Koreans can only afford the simplest and most basic foods. While a few people have the money to dine at Pyongyang's restaurants, many more do not get enough to eat and suffer from malnutrition—especially in the wake of the famine of the 1990s.

In more prosperous times, however, Korean diners do enjoy a rich variety of dishes. The main food at all meals is white rice, cooked alone or with other grains. Kimchi (pickled cabbage and other vegetables), often prepared to be extremely spicy, is another standard. Along with rice, kimchi is almost always present on a Korean table. Popular seasonings such as soy sauce, soybean paste, red pepper, gingerroot, and sesame oil and seeds add flavor to Korean foods.

Vegetarian dishes featuring grains, vegetables, and tofu (made from soybeans) have long been popular in Korea, especially since meat has often been scarce due to limited grazing land and other limitations. When meat is available, chicken is most commonly eaten, along with fish, while beef is the most popular red meat. Beef is the main ingredient in the famous *bulgogi,* a dish of beef strips marinated in soy sauce, sesame seeds, pepper, onion, and garlic, and broiled over a charcoal fire. A popular North Korean specialty is Pyongyang *raengmyon,* a dish of buckwheat noodles served in a cold beef broth. The dish is some-

KOREAN COLD NOODLES

Raengmyon recipes vary depending on a cook's personal tastes and what ingredients are available, but here is one version of the chilled noodle soup loved by North Koreans.

8 cups canned beef stock

1 teaspoon vinegar

1 clove garlic, minced or grated

1 teaspoon white sugar

1 teaspoon black pepper

1 teaspoon soy sauce, or to taste

½ pound pork loin

1 pound uncooked buckwheat noodles

1 Asian pear, cut into thin wedges or matchsticks

1 cucumber, thinly sliced or cut into matchsticks

2 hard-boiled eggs, cut in half

2 pickled white radishes (also called daikon, or Chinese white radish), cut into matchsticks (optional)

1. In a large stockpot, combine beef stock, vinegar, garlic, sugar, black pepper, and soy sauce. Bring this broth to a simmer over medium-low heat and cook 20 minutes, stirring occasionally. Remove from heat and allow broth to cool. Transfer to refrigerator to chill for at least 2 hours.
2. Fill a large pot or saucepan with water and add pork loin. Bring to a boil over high heat and cook 15 minutes, or until meat is cooked all the way through. Remove from heat and set aside. When meat is cool enough to handle, slice it into thin slices and discard water.
3. Bring a large saucepan of water to a boil over high heat and add noodles. Cook 3 minutes, stirring constantly. Remove from heat, rinse with cold running water until noodles are cold, and drain.
4. Divide noodles among four bowls. Pour chilled broth over noodles and top decoratively with sliced pork, pear, cucumber, eggs, and radishes (if using). Serve with ice cubes if desired.

Serves 4

times topped with hard-boiled eggs, sliced pears, pieces of meat, or vegetables. Another local favorite is *onban*, an entrée of steamed white rice in a warm broth and often garnished with green onions, sliced chicken, and other toppings.

Like food and other resources in North Korea, clothing was once distributed by the government. As economic changes have occurred, many citizens have had the chance to buy their own. However, the struggling economy has also led to clothing shortages. Some aid agencies have reported that many citizens do not have adequate clothes, especially for different seasons.

However, highly prized traditional Korean clothing, called *chosun-ot*, does appear for some special occasions. The chosun-ot dates back to the second century A.D. Typically, the chosun-ot worn by women consists of the *chima* (a long wraparound skirt), paired with a *jeogori* (a short jacket or blouse tied in front with long ribbons). Men wear wide-sleeved jackets called jeogori, pairing them with baggy trousers fitted at the waist and ankles. Sometimes Korean men also wear long overcoats. Historically, wealthy Koreans wore brightly-colored silken chosun-ot, while the common people wore clothes of cotton or hemp and were limited to white, gray, or other muted colors. In modern North Korea, chosun-ot are generally limited to public figures such as tour guides, dancers, singers, and other performers of traditional arts.

One item worn by every North Korean is a badge, usually pinned over the heart, showing Kim Il Sung, Kim Jong-il, or both. Variations in badge design indicate the rank of the wearer, and citizens are required to display these pins when in public, while outsiders are generally forbidden to wear or own them.

To learn more about North Korean culture, go to www.vgsbooks.com for links.

◉ Visual Arts

Among the earliest artworks found in Korea are murals that were painted on the walls of tombs more than 1,500 years ago. Depictions of birds, animals, and human figures in the paintings of ancient Koguryo (in present-day North Korea) are especially lively and colorful.

One of Korea's most outstanding crafts has always been ceramics. The celadon porcelain of the Koryo period (936–1392) was adorned with intricate designs of birds, flowers, and other figures. Later pottery was simpler than celadon but still widely admired. During the Chosun dynasty, Confucianism and Chinese culture became the primary influence on the Korean arts, and scholars produced Chinese poetry, calligraphy (ornate handwriting), and landscape paintings. In addition, a uniquely Korean style of painting developed during this period among less-educated Koreans. These folk paintings depicted the daily life of common Korean people, and some reflected traditional Korean shamanism by portraying nature gods.

Despite this rich history, modern North Korean art has been restricted. The government and the KWP monitor and control artistic output very carefully. Artists are instructed to create only works that depict the successes and glory of the Communist system, the Korean people, and the Kim family, and which usually take the form of propaganda posters or billboards. In addition to these, the most prominent examples of visual art in North Korea are public monuments and architecture. Pyongyang, in particular, is home to many massive statues of Kim Il Sung and Kim Jong-il, as well as monuments depicting historical scenes and representing Communist ideals.

North Korean architecture also reflects the country's political and cultural history. Enormous modern government buildings, apartment buildings, stadiums, and other structures display Communist architectural traits such as imposing brick or concrete faces, vast plazas, and signs with Communist sayings and symbols. Other buildings, such as museums and libraries, show more traditional Korean influences and may have tiled roofs, sloping eaves, and gardens.

Literature and Film

Historically, Korean literature developed on two separate social levels. Scholars and wealthy writers composed poetry, while most other people cherished tales and songs. Among the yangban, a short lyric poem known as the *sijo* arose in the twelfth century and still occupies a distinctive place in Korean literature. These simple, expressive poems describe the beauty of nature, enjoyment of life, and philosophical thoughts.

Among common people, myths and legends inspired *pansori*, which are long ballads chanted by a traveling minstrel to drum accompaniment. Three of the best-known pansori are *The Tale of Simchung*, about a devoted daughter who helps to restore her blind father's sight; *The Tale of Chunhyang*, a love story; and *The Tale of Hungbu and Nolbu*, about a virtuous younger brother and his wicked older brother.

Contemporary North Korean literature, like the visual arts, has been limited by the government. Authors celebrate juche, the Kims, and Communism. Other common themes are the description of North Korea as a workers' paradise where all citizens are happy and equal or tales of the envy and respect that people in other countries feel for the citizens of North Korea. Two authors who became prominent for such works in the early years of the DPRK were Han Sor-ya and Lee Ki-yong. Kim Il Sung was also said to have written several novels, along with many political speeches and essays. However, the novels, in particular—which include *The Sea of Blood* and *The Song of Korea*—are suspected by many scholars to have been ghostwritten (written by an unnamed author and published under Kim's name).

Film is another art that is practiced in North Korea, but with strict limitations. Kim Jong-il is said to be a fan of Hollywood movies and to hire English speakers to translate them into Korean. However, average North Koreans are not permitted to view U.S. films or other outside media. Instead, a variety of propaganda films are produced and shown within the country. These works usually praise Kim Il Sung or Kim Jong-il, tell inspiring stories of Communist and revolutionary heroes in North Korean history, or idealize life in North Korea. One such film is *On the Green Carpet* (2001), which centers on a coach preparing young performers for the May Day show in Pyongyang. The movie praises the willingness of the children to work as hard as necessary to please Kim Jong-il with a good performance and presents North Korean life as pleasant and with few troubles.

> In the wind
> that blew last night,
> Peach blossoms fell,
> scattered in the garden.
> A boy came out with a broom,
> Intending to sweep them away.
> No, do not sweep them away,
> no, no.
> Are fallen flowers
> not flowers?"
>
> —A sijo by an anonymous Korean poet, undated

The traditional mask dance originated during the Koryo dynasty. It became popular again in the late nineteenth century, and in the early twenty-first century, the DPRK issued three postage stamps honoring the age-old art.

◉ Music and Dance

Like much of North Korean culture, its music and dance draw on many sources, with roots in Confucian rituals, court music, Buddhist chants, and folk music. Some court music dates back to the Silla era of the A.D. 600s or earlier, while ancient Confucian music is believed to be even older. Court music is slow, solemn, and complex, and its dances are stately and formal. In contrast to the solemn court songs, folk music is usually fast and lively, with irregular rhythms, and it is often accompanied by energetic dancing.

While traditional music and dance performances are sometimes held, most are viewed primarily by party officials and tourists. The music available to the general public is primarily "revolutionary" music. Hymnlike songs praise North Korea and the Kim family, while revolutionary operas tell dramatic, emotional stories usually related to Kim Il Sung's guerrilla war against the Japanese or to the success of the juche idea. The music and style of these operas draw upon ch'anggeuk (traditional Korean opera), as well as upon old folk songs. Although advertised by the government as entirely Korean in origin, they sometimes also borrow themes from Western classical music. In addition, circus troupes of acrobats, horseback riders, magicians, and other performers also stage impressive and highly athletic shows.

◉ Sports

North Koreans consider athletic activity very important, and children are encouraged to exercise and to play sports. Activities range from traditional to modern games and include both individual and team sports. Children also practice the gymnastics that they will show off on May Day and other special events.

Some of the most popular sports in North Korea are actually of Western origin. The British introduced soccer to Korea in 1882, and despite the nation's modern aversion to outside influence, the sport remains popular. Other activities include baseball, volleyball, basketball, skiing, skating, swimming, and table tennis. However, most North Koreans do not have very much leisure time to participate in sports, and people who do are usually professional athletes. Those who excel are honored with special titles, the highest being People's Sportsman or Sportswoman. These stars are seen as national heroes and are often given special treatment by the government.

At the Olympics and other international competitions, North Korean teams typically perform well in sports such as gymnastics and weight lifting. When these athletic teams travel abroad to take part in international sports competitions, a three-hundred-woman cheerleading squad often accompanies them. Attractive, identically dressed, and performing chants, cheers, and choreographed routines in perfect unison, the cheerleaders have proven to be very popular abroad—often drawing more attention than the sports events themselves. In addition to encouraging their teams, they act as representatives of the DPRK, praising Kim Jong-il and North Korea enthusiastically and proclaiming hope for reunification.

Many North Korean athletes are skilled in the martial arts, and Taekwondo is one of Korea's best-known traditional sports. This two-thousand-year-old self-defense martial art uses rapid punches and kicks, and its name is usually translated as "the way of hand and foot." *Ssireum*, another ancient Korean art, is a form of wrestling that is at least 1,500 years old and is considered a national sport.

The **North Korean cheerleading squad** performs at a men's basketball game against the Philippines at the 2002 Asian Games in Busan, South Korea. Their tightly guarded living quarters during the game were on a 9,770-ton (8,861-metric-ton) ferry docked nearby.

THE ECONOMY

By the end of the Korean War, years of occupation and conflict had seriously disrupted North Korea's economy. Bombing, napalm, and fire had badly scarred the country, damaging farmland and factories and leaving much of the workforce disabled. In addition, maintaining the large Korean People's Army remained a heavy drain on the nation's financial resources.

However, with division most of the peninsula's natural resources were in the North, and before that the Japanese had focused their industries in the northern part of the peninsula. The DPRK built on these foundations after the Korean War, jump-starting land reform and rapid industrial development. The government also introduced a series of economic plans designed to reach output goals within specified time limits. Using these strategies, North Korea experienced significant economic growth and a greatly increased standard of living in its early days.

Progress slowed somewhat after the initial surge but continued to various degrees through the following decades. By the 1990s, however, the economy had begun to struggle due to factors including the 1991 collapse of the Soviet Union—a Communist North Korean ally. Government distribution of food, clothing, and other resources faltered, and a flourishing black market (illegal trade) arose.

North Korea's strict program of self-reliance, combined with state ownership of nearly all businesses, land, and other assets, gave its economy little flexibility to deal with such challenges, but leaders had vowed never to compromise juche or Communism. Nevertheless, in 1991 North Korea cautiously established a "free economic and trade zone" in the sister cities of Rajin and Sonbong, hoping to revive the nation's struggling economy. Foreign investment in the zone was encouraged, and a controlled amount of trade with outside nations was permitted. However, limited funds hindered the experiment's development.

Meanwhile, challenges continued to batter the economy. In 1993 KWP leaders announced that the most recent economic strategy—a Seven-Year Plan that had begun in 1987—had not met its goals. Kim Il Sung's death in 1994 was yet another blow, followed by disastrous floods that hit the nation in 1994, 1995, and 1996, wiping out agricultural areas and damaging cities and villages. The flooding was followed by widespread famine, and economic and living standards plummeted while malnutrition and related diseases soared. In addition, the nation's infrastructure—basic systems such as energy, transportation, and communications—began to crumble, as funds to maintain it vanished. Fuel and power shortages set in. International economic sanctions (penalties), imposed because of the nuclear crisis, further crippled the country.

The 2000 summit between Kim Jong-il and Kim Dae-jung seemed to signal a more open North Korea, and economic developments soon followed. Although the Rajin-Sonbong project had so far failed to prosper, in 2002 North Korean leaders tried a similar attempt to revive the economy. Inspired by Chinese reforms, they announced the establishment of a Special Administrative Region (SAR) in Sinuiju, near the Chinese border. The SAR was intended to function as a separate, capitalist region, complete with its own government and administration—some members of which would not be Korean—and would seek investment from China and other countries to build and run factories and businesses. Although disagreement between China and North Korea, along with ongoing global tensions, threaten to undo the project, many observers still hope that it will succeed.

These changes were paired with the gradual opening of markets and shops selling food and other items, including some products made outside North Korea. These places gave North Koreans the chance to buy goods that the government was no longer reliably providing and encouraged a limited amount of free-market activity. Although price reforms in 2002 raised the cost of goods, wages increased as well. As these changes slowly took hold, the economy also slowly began to grow again.

Industry and Trade

At its founding, the DPRK began working toward rapid industrialization. Over the next decades, North Korean factories cranked out products including textiles, machinery, cement, and chemicals. The nation also rose to be among the world's top producers of weapons. However, like all parts of the country's economy, industry took a hit in the 1990s, and many factories closed due to a lack of power, raw materials, and money for maintenance.

Nevertheless, industry still accounts for about 38 percent of the gross domestic product, or GDP (the total annual value of goods and services produced within the country's borders), and employs an estimated one-third of the workforce. In addition, growing interaction between North Korea and the global economy has led to the prospects of joint business ventures. Trade with South Korea also rose after the 2000

North Korean factories that stayed open in the late 1990s were estimated to be running at only 10 to 15 percent of their full potential.

summit. While North Korea still suffers from a trade deficit—importing more than it exports—the special zones established in Rajin-Sonbong and Sinuiju are hoped to help address this problem eventually. In the meantime, North Korea exports goods including textiles and machinery, and its major trading partners are South Korea, China, Japan, India, and Hong Kong.

Military Spending and Weapons Production

It is estimated that more than one million North Koreans are in the Korean People's Army, the nation's military, making it a very significant employer. In addition, millions more are members of reserve forces such as the Worker-Peasant Red Guards. In all, an estimated one-quarter to one-third of the nation's GDP is spent on the military. While army life is reputed to be harsh, soldiers are thought to be guaranteed a certain amount of food each day—a significant benefit in North Korea.

All high school and college students receive some military training, and physically able men are required to do three to five years of military service, usually beginning at age seventeen. In the past, exceptions have been made for reasons such as family background, college attendance, or the possession of technical knowledge or other skills seen as valuable to the republic. However, in 2002 the country began revamping the system to make more people eligible for service. Since the early 2000s, more women have also joined the military. In the past, they had not been required to serve but could volunteer for certain posts. However, outside observers believe that North Korea may have begun drafting women, also. Some theorize that the apparent military buildup has been in response to rising tensions between the DPRK and the United States.

In addition, weapons production is one of North Korea's largest industries. The nation is believed to have sold missiles and other weapons or military materials to Iran, Pakistan, and other nations in the Middle East, as well as in Africa. In May 2004, UN officials learned that North Korea had also sold uranium to Libya in the past, probably for use in making nuclear weapons.

Agriculture, Forestry, and Fishing

Little of North Korea's land is arable (suitable for farming), which has always limited its farming. In modern times, agriculture accounts for about 25 to 30 percent of the GDP and employs about one-third of the workforce. Even the land that is planted with crops is mostly mountainous, and the rough terrain has made mechanized equipment difficult to use. Nevertheless, the government has worked hard to increase productivity by introducing the use of machinery wherever possible. When the economy began to struggle in the 1990s, shortages of fuel to run the machines turned back the clock as farmers once more worked the fields by hand. Many industrial workers—put out of work by factory closings—also joined agricultural teams. The situation only worsened as peasants struggling to feed their families overfarmed hillside areas, causing deforestation and erosion that helped contribute to the flooding of the late 1990s.

Beginning in 2000, the government launched programs to address the food shortage by increasing crop yields and adding more variety to plantings. Although most of North Korea's farmland had been dedicated to growing rice and corn, the nation's two principal grains, other crops including potatoes, barley, and wheat were given new attention. International groups also donated fertilizer, seeds, and additional aid to help increase output.

Other food crops in the country include cabbages and soybeans. Some farmers also raise livestock such as chickens, pigs, cattle, goats, and rabbits, although grain shortages have hurt the populations of these animals. However, by 2001, as the economy in general began to slowly climb, agricultural production grew slightly as well.

Much of North Korea's nonarable land is covered with forests. In the northern mountains, especially, these forests produce valuable pine, spruce, fir, and larch. Although the nation's forest cover has

Workers harvest rice by hand from this field between Pyongyang and Kaesung. Chronic fuel shortages force many North Koreans to farm this way.

been thinned by clearing for farm-land and timber over the years, refor-estation programs are in place to combat the loss.

Fishing also contributes to the North Korean economy. With a fleet of an estimated forty thousand deep-sea vessels and smaller boats, North Korean fishing crews sail from major ports including Nampo, Chongjin, Wonsan, and Hungnam. Deep-sea crews primarily bring in herring, mackerel, pike, and yellowtail. Boats in closer coastal waters pull in eels and shrimp from the Yellow Sea, while the East Sea yields octo-pus, pollock, anchovies, sardines, and cod.

Service Sector

About one-third of North Korea's GDP is estimated to come from the service sector, which also employs one-quarter or more of its workforce. In the past, most of the nation's service workers held jobs at state-run shops or in other parts of the nation's food and clothing distribution systems. However, as the North Korean economy struggled to over-come famine and other pressures, more and more people have found work at the independent markets and shops that have begun to appear around the country.

Others are employed by the still limited but growing tourism industry. Many serve as guides, as visitors are never permitted to travel alone, either in Pyongyang or beyond. Hotel and restaurant workers also provide services to tourists, as well as to wealthy and influential North Koreans.

Infrastructure

The difficult years of the 1990s took their toll on many aspects of North Korea's infrastructure. Energy systems were perhaps the hard-est hit. North Korea had worked hard to become self-sufficient in terms of power and nearly achieved that goal by building hydroelec-tric and thermal (coal-burning) power plants. However, the nation still needed to import petroleum to fully meet its energy and fuel

Catch up on the latest news from North Korea. Visit www.vgsbooks.com for links.

needs and had not yet gained working nuclear plants. After the economic crisis of the 1990s—with petroleum shipments cut off due to the nuclear crisis, hydroelectric facilities damaged by floods, and coal reserves running low—widespread power shortages and blackouts became commonplace.

Transportation has fared slightly better. Although most citizens still get around on foot or by bicycle, the number of North Koreans owning cars began to rise in the early 2000s as more goods became available. Pyongyang residents use the city's tram (streetcar) and subway systems. Outside of cities, travel is tightly controlled, and residents wishing to move through the country need the government's permission before doing so. However, a public transit network does provide transportation within and between cities. Buses and trains run on more than 19,000 miles (30,577 km) of roads and 3,000 miles (4,828 km) of track crisscrossing the country. Further expansion of both expressways and railway tracks is also planned, including projects to complete travel routes across the DMZ, linking the North and South. North Korea's national airline, Air Koryo, flies out of airports in Pyongyang and other cities, making trips to other destinations in Asia as well as less frequent flights to Europe, the Middle East, and Africa.

The Pyongyang subway is famous for its ornate decoration and impressive architecture. Stations and stops are adorned with glittering lights, stained-glass windows, bronze plaques, and large mosaic murals made from thousands of tiny tiles. Each station's decorations also reflect a different theme, such as "Victory," "Liberation," or "Golden Fields." Even the light fixtures contribute to the theme—for example, chandeliers in the "Golden Fields" station are bunches of small colored globes, meant to look like grapes.

Communication is tightly controlled by the DPRK's government, which carefully monitors and limits information entering and leaving the nation. Television, radio, and newspapers are state-run and are believed to distribute mainly propaganda and censored information. Although cell phones became available for the first time in 2002, in 2004 officials banned them for unspecified reasons. And while plans have been made to expand Internet and World Wide Web access, many observers remain skeptical that changes will actually take effect. In the past, some residents have been allowed to use internal e-mail, though they could only view a few government-controlled websites. Even with broader access—which will probably only be affordable for the wealthiest North Koreans—information is still likely to be restricted.

The Future

Under Communist rule, North Korea initially experienced a rise in industry, agricultural output, and standards of living. However, the nation's extreme secrecy and isolation, strict dictatorship, and violations of human rights—combined with natural disasters, poor international relations, and other challenges—left the nation struggling in the early 2000s.

Despite the challenges, many observers hope that the gradual opening of North Korea's market will eventually improve life for the country's citizens. Others fear that it may only widen the gap between rich and poor. And, even as Kim Jong-il agrees to limited reforms, he also continues to avoid making changes that might threaten the government's control. In any case, until North Koreans can obtain greater human rights and develop resources, the nation's future success remains uncertain. But beneath its current troubles, it holds great riches in culture, history, and character. If and when the Hermit Kingdom does open to the world and join the global community, it will have much to offer.

OPENING THE DOORS

In addition to economic reforms, North Korea has made other moves toward greater openness at various times over the last decades. One of the first big events was the 13th World Festival of Youth and Students, which welcomed young people from more than one hundred countries to Pyongyang in July 1989. In April 1995, the capital city opened up for the International Sports and Cultural Festival for Peace, and in 2002, Pyongyang invited a global audience to its annual April Spring Friendship Art Festival, which that year celebrated Kim Il Sung's ninetieth birthday and lasted for two months. Although foreign visitors still had limited freedom to travel within the country, each of these events marked an important widening of the door into North Korea.

Timeline

4000 B.C.	Early evidence of human civilization exists in Korea.
2333 B.C.	According to Korean legend, Dan-gun founds Korea.
108 B.C.	The Chinese Han dynasty conquers northern Korea.
A.D. 200s	The Baekje and Silla kingdoms form.
372	Buddhism arrives in Korea by way of China. Korea's first Dae-hak (university) is founded.
668	Silla unifies the Korea Peninsula.
EARLY 900s	Silla fragments.
936	Wang Keon reunifies the peninsula under a new kingdom called Koryo.
993-1018	Koryo clashes with Manchuria.
1170	Military leaders rebel and seize control of Koryo.
1231	Mongol warriors attack Koryo.
1392	Yi Song-gye seizes the Koryo throne and founds the Chosun dynasty.
1400s	Confucianism spreads in Korea.
1418-1450	King Sejong rules.
1440s	Hangul is invented.
1592	Japan attacks Korea.
1597	Japan attacks again.
1627	Chinese forces attack Korea.
1636	Chinese forces strike Korea again.
1785	Catholic missionaries arrive in Korea.
1876	Japan opens Korea's markets to trade.
1894	Demonstrations against the government erupt into the Donghak Rebellion, which then escalates into the Sino-Japanese War.
1910	Japan claims Korea as a colony.
1919	The March First Movement takes place.
1920s	Korean Communists become active from bases in China and the Soviet Union.
1941	World War II breaks out in East Asia.

1945   Japan is defeated in World War II. The United States and the Soviet Union divide Korea into southern and northern states.

1946   The Provisional People's Committee is founded in Pyongyang with Kim Il Sung at its head.

1948   The Democratic People's Republic of Korea is founded, led by Kim Il Sung.

1950   North Korea invades South Korea. The Korean War begins.

1951   Truce talks begin among nations involved in the Korean War.

1953   A cease-fire ends fighting in the Korean War.

1960s   North Korea industrializes rapidly.

1970s   Food and fuel shortages begin to plague North Korea.

1981–1983   Worker uprisings are put down by force.

1989   North Korea hosts the 13th World Festival of Youth and Students in Pyongyang.

1991   The Rajin-Sonbong free economic and trade zone is established.

1993   In response to accusations of nuclear weapons development, North Korean leaders announce the country's withdrawal from the Nuclear Non-Proliferation Treaty (NPT). They later cancel their withdrawal and remain in the NPT.

1994   Kim Il Sung dies. Severe flooding strikes, and famine soon takes hold of the country.

1995   North Korea hosts the International Sports and Cultural Festival for Peace.

2000   Kim Jong-il meets with South Korean president Kim Dae-jung in Pyongyang.

2002   North Korea announces plans for a Special Administrative Region at Sinuiju.

2004   Six-nation talks begin in hopes of settling the nuclear crisis. A train accident in Ryongchon forces the government to call for outside aid. UN officials confirm that North Korea has sold uranium to Libya. A North-South agreement is reached to reduce propaganda and improve relations between the nations. More than four hundred North Korean defectors are admitted to South Korea.

COUNTRY NAME Democratic People's Republic of Korea

AREA 46,541 square miles (120,541 sq. km)

MAIN LANDFORMS Hamgyong Mountains, Nangnim Mountains, Taebaek Mountains, Myohyang Mountains, Myohyangsan, Kwanmobong, Puksubaeksan, Nangnimsan, Kumgangsan

HIGHEST POINT Baekdusan, 9,020 feet (2,749 m) above sea level

LOWEST POINT Sea level

MAJOR RIVERS Amnok, Tumen, Daedong, and Chongchon

ANIMALS Siberian black bears, Siberian tigers, wild boars, Amur leopards, Amur gorals

CAPITAL CITY Pyongyang

OTHER MAJOR CITIES Nampo, Hamhung, Chongjin, Wonsan, and Hyangsan

OFFICIAL LANGUAGE Korean

MONETARY UNIT Won. 1 won = 100 chon.

NORTH KOREAN CURRENCY

North Korea's official currency is the won. However, until distribution systems began to break down in the 1990s, average citizens used mostly government-distributed ration tickets to obtain goods. While the won is used more widely in the 2000s, its value remains very low. Euros, the currency of the European Union, are used for all foreign transactions. The exchange rate is officially 1 euro to about 170 won, but a thriving black market makes the true rate closer to 1 euro to 1,500 won or higher. Won bills and coins show Kim Il Sung and Kim Jong-il, sites of national importance such as Kim Il Sung's birthplace, wildlife and nature scenes, and Communist themes such as workers and students.

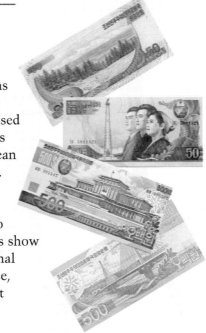

North Korea's flag was adopted in 1948. It displays bands of blue, white, and red, with a white circle surrounding a red five-pointed star lying in the left part of the red field. Although multiple interpretations of the flag's meaning exist, a common version states that the blue bands represent independence and peace, the white bands represent purity and strength, and the red band and star stand for Communism and the KWP.

Chosen to represent the nation in 1947, the national anthem of North Korea is "Achimun Pinnara," or "Let Morning Shine." Also called simply "Patriotic Song," the anthem has lyrics by Pak Se Yong (1902–1989) and music by Kim Won Gyun (b. 1917). An English translation of the lyrics follows below.

Achimun Pinnara (Let Morning Shine)
Let morning shine on the silver and gold of this land,
Three thousand leagues packed with natural wealth.
My beautiful fatherland.
The glory of a wise people
Brought up in a culture brilliant
With a history five millennia long.
Let us devote our bodies and minds
To supporting this Korea for ever.

The firm will, bonded with truth,
Nest for the spirit of labor,
Embracing the atmosphere of Mount Paektu [Baekdusan],
Will go forth to all the world.
The country established by the will of the people,
Breasting the raging waves with soaring strength.
Let us glorify for ever this Korea,
Limitlessly rich and strong.

For a link to a site where you can listen to North Korea's national anthem, "Let Morning Shine," visit www.vgsbooks.com.

The following names are written and alphabetized in the traditional Korean order, with the family name first.

CHUNG JU-YOUNG (1915–2001) Born in the far north of the Korea Peninsula, Chung was the first of eight children in a farming family. He labored on the railroad, at the docks, and in the fields. Desperate to escape poverty, Chung once sold his family's only cow and used the money to run away to Seoul. In 1946 he opened the Hyundai Motor Industrial Company in Seoul, which expanded into construction work. After the Korean War, Hyundai rebuilt roads and bridges in the South—and then built cars to drive on them. However, Chung never forgot his northern roots. Throughout his career, he worked to improve North-South relations and to encourage investment in the North.

KING GWANGGAETO (374–413) Gwanggaeto—also called Gwanggaeto the Great—became ruler of Koguryo in 391. Just seventeen years old when he took the throne, Gwanggaeto had soon greatly expanded the northern realm's territory. He was said to have conquered more than one thousand cities and villages during his reign, which—despite all of this war—was known as Yeongnak, or "Eternal Rejoicing." Gwanggaeto also encouraged the spread of Buddhism, directing the building of nine temples in Pyongyang. The king's tomb is believed to lie in Jian, China, just across the Amnok River.

HAN SOR-YA (1900–?) Although little is known of Han Sor-ya's life, he was an influential figure in the early years of the DPRK, acting as one of the major writers who helped to establish the cult of personality surrounding Kim Il Sung. With works such as *Jackals*, a short novel from 1951 demonizing Americans, Han also spread propaganda praising the North Korean government and criticizing others.

HONG SEOK-JUNG (b. 1941) Born in Seoul, Hong moved to North Korea with his family in 1948. Like his grandfather Hong Myong-hi, he writes historical novels. Hong's 2002 novel *Hwang Jin Yi* tells the story of a Chosun-era female entertainer and explores social issues rather than focusing on the Kim family. In 2004 the novel came out in South Korea, and that July it won the Manhae Prize for Literature. Awarded by a South Korean publisher for outstanding Korean-language works, the prize had never before been won by a North Korean author.

KIM IL SUNG (1912–1994) Born Kim Song-ju in Pyongyang, Kim Il Sung has a murky biography, as official DPRK accounts and outside evidence often conflict. Sources largely agree on the fact that, as a young man, Kim fought in the anti-Japanese resistance and the Communist guerrilla movement in Manchuria (in modern China) and the Soviet Union—although opinions differ on how central Kim's role was. After World War II, stories diverge further. International historians believe that Soviet leaders chose Kim as a figurehead for the new nation, while DPRK sources state that Kim founded the DPRK, KWP, and Korean People's Army and was elected president by the people. Kim ruled as dictator of Communist North Korea for more than forty years, elevating himself to almost godlike status through an intense propaganda campaign.

KIM JONG-IL (b. ca. 1941) Like his father's story, Kim Jong-il's life story has several versions. DPRK lore states that he was born on Baekdusan in 1942, while outside sources believe that he was born in 1941 in a guerrilla camp in the Soviet Union. As Kim Il Sung's eldest son, Kim Jong-il was chosen to lead North Korea. However, he has never achieved the popularity or hero status of Kim Il Sung. Said to be an irresponsible partygoer as a youth, he continues to have a reputation for extravagant behavior, such as employing troupes of private entertainers or sending cooks around the world to buy specialty foods. Kim Jong-il also differs from his father in that, while largely maintaining North Korea's isolation and Communist system, he has also begun moving slowly toward reforms. Kim is eventually expected to transfer power to one of his own sons.

KIM YONG (b. ca. 1950) Growing up in the North during the Korean War, Kim was separated from his parents and sent to an orphanage. Despite troubled beginnings, Kim built a promising career in the North Korean Intelligence Agency, the military, and the KWP. However, when he came up for a promotion in 1993, a background check revealed that his father had been executed on charges of spying. Arrested and sent to a hard-labor camp as a political prisoner, Kim endured the camp's harsh conditions until his escape to China in 1998. Kim moved to South Korea and became an advocate for human rights in North Korea.

KYE SUN HEE (b. 1979) Born in Pyongyang, Kye began practicing the martial art of judo at a young age. Competing at the 1996 Summer Olympic Games in Atlanta, Georgia, Kye won a surprise victory over the Japanese judo champion, earning a gold medal at just sixteen years old. The win propelled her to fame at home, where she was awarded the title of People's Sportswoman and received honors and gifts. She has gone on to earn many more medals, including gold medals at two World Judo Championships and a bronze medal at the 2000 Olympics.

LEE SUNG KI (1905–1996) After studying in Japan and working at a Seoul university, Lee moved to North Korea during the Korean War and became one of the nation's most prominent scientists. Highly praised by Kim Il Sung, Lee was made director of North Korea's Atomic Energy Agency, putting him in charge of the nation's nuclear program. Lee is also said to have worked on developing biological and chemical weapons. Since Lee's death, he has been the subject of international accusations regarding weapons testing on prisoners. During his lifetime, however, the North Korean government considered him a national hero.

North Korea is a fascinating nation with a long history and a landscape of striking natural beauty. However, tense international relations make it a difficult and possibly even dangerous tourist destination. The government strictly regulates travel and sometimes closes the country to outsiders. Because the United States and North Korea do not maintain diplomatic relations, it is especially hard for U.S. travelers to visit. Anyone considering going to North Korea should check with the U.S. State Department to learn more. Go to www.vgsbooks.com for a link.

BAEKDUSAN North Korea's most famous mountain—and the legendary birthplace of Dan-gun—offers stunning natural scenery and hiking trails, as well as hotels for weary travelers. Visitors can stop to see a small log cabin advertised as the site of Kim Jong-il's birth, and no one will want to miss the beauty of Lake Cheonji at the mountain's top.

DMZ The Demilitarized Zone—which, despite its name, is actually very heavily guarded—offers an up-close look at the remains of the Cold War and at the ongoing division between the Koreas. The town of Kichong-dong (meaning "Peace Village") lies in the North Korean half of the DMZ, inhabited by a few select residents. In the center of the zone is Panmunjeom, a village in which peace talks took place at the end of the Korean War and where subsequent inter-Korea talks have also been held.

KAESUNG This ancient Korean capital, dating back to the A.D. 900s, is the site of some of North Korea's richest historical architecture, including bridges, temples, pagodas, and pavilions. The large Seonggyungwan Academy, established as a national Confucian university in the 1000s, has been transformed into the Koryo Museum and displays a wealth of historical artifacts. Other nearby attractions are the Tomb of King Kongmin and the Pakyeon Falls.

KUMGANGSAN One of North Korea's many mountains, Kumgangsan is one of the few places in the country officially open to tourism. Supervised tours to the mountain take visitors up to its heights for a spectacular view. Hikers will notice that many rock faces are carved with hangul letters. Painted red, these messages communicate slogans such as "Long live comrade Kim Il Sung" and "General Kim Jong-il, the great commander born of heaven."

PYONGYANG The capital city offers many sights to visitors. Major monuments include the Arch of Triumph, the Tower of the Juche Idea, and the Mansudae Grand Monument, all reflecting events in North Korean history or praising Kim Il Sung or Kim Jong-il. Kim Il Sung is said to have been born in the humble cottage still standing in the Mangyeongdae district, regarded as the "Cradle of the Revolution." At the Kumsusan Memorial Palace, Kim Il Sung's embalmed body is on view. Gardens, parks, theaters, a zoo, and a popular circus also provide entertainment.

Buddhism: a religion founded in India by the monk Siddhartha Gautama (Buddha) in the 500s B.C. Subsequently, the Chinese brought Buddhist scriptures to Korea, and Buddhism gained a following in Korea between the 300s and 500s A.D.

Chondogyo: meaning "Religion of the Heavenly Way," a faith that appeared in nineteenth-century Korea and blended ideas from Confucianism, Buddhism, and Christianity into one belief system. Like other religions in North Korea, Chondogyo is believed to have followers who practice it in secret.

Communism: a political and economic model based on the idea of common, rather than private, property. In a Communist system, the government controls all goods and theoretically distributes them equally among citizens.

Confucianism: a system of ethics based on the teachings of the Chinese philosopher Confucius, who emphasized morality and proper conduct in all aspects of life. Confucianism also arranges society into rigid classes.

Demilitarized Zone (DMZ): an area that was set up after the Korean War to serve as a buffer zone between the two Koreas. Guards on both sides of the DMZ—which is a 2.4-mile-wide (3.9-km) strip of land along the 38th Parallel—strictly control access to the area.

Donghak: a movement founded in the mid-1800s by Choe Je-u. Translated as "Eastern learning," Donghak combined religion, philosophy, and politics and blended ancient Confucian and Buddhist ideas with modern thought. Its goals included keeping Korea free of foreign influence, ending government corruption, and providing more opportunities for farmers.

dynasty: a ruling family. Within dynasties, power is usually handed down from fathers to sons, and one dynasty may remain in control for hundreds of years. North Korea is said to have the world's first Communist dynasty, as Communist leadership is usually unrelated to family ties.

juche: a philosophy of self-reliance. Kim Il Sung made the idea of juche the guiding idea behind his rule and the government of North Korea.

propaganda: ideas or information spread—often by a government—to enforce a desired mindset and to strengthen the control of one party or system. North Korean propaganda praises the nation's leaders, its Communist system, and its culture, while criticizing those of other nations, especially the capitalist United States and, to a lesser degree, the former colonial power Japan.

Sirhak: translated as "practical learning," Sirhak emphasized the value of Korean history and culture in solving the modern state's problems, while also pursuing Western thought

United Nations: an international organization formed at the end of World War II in 1945 to help handle global disputes. The United Nations replaced a similar, earlier group known as the League of Nations.

Western: a geographic and political term that usually refers to the politics, culture, and history of the United States and Europe

yangban: a wealthy class of highly educated scholar-officials who were powerful during the Chosun dynasty (1392–1910)

Ash, Robert F. "The Democratic People's Republic of Korea: Economy." In *Regional Surveys of the World: The Far East and Australasia,* pp. 666–676. London: Europa Publications, 2002.
This article examines North Korea's recent economic situation.

Cable News Network. *CNN.com International—Asia.* 2004.
<http://edition.cnn.com/ASIA/> (April 23, 2004).
This site provides current events and breaking news about North Korea, as well as a searchable archive of older articles.

Connor, Mary E. *The Koreas: A Global Studies Handbook.* Santa Barbara, CA: ABC-CLIO, 2002.
This comprehensive text touches on topics from geography to shamanism, offering an informative and helpful introduction to North Korea.

Cumings, Bruce. *Korea's Place in the Sun: A Modern History.* New York: W. W. Norton and Company, 1997.
This detailed look at Korea's history, evolution, and future is a useful introduction to the country.

———. *North Korea: Another Country.* New York: New Press, 2004.
This history and analysis of North Korea offers a new perspective on the nation and its place in the world.

Europa World Yearbook, 2003. Vol. 2. London: Europa Publications, 2003.
Covering North Korea's recent history, economy, and government, this annual publication also provides a wealth of statistics on population, employment, trade, and more.

Foster-Carter, Aidan. *Aidan Foster-Carter.* 2003.
<http://www.aidanfc.net/> (April 23, 2004).
This website presents articles by a British writer who has devoted his career to the study and analysis of North Korea. The site also offers links to other valuable information about North Korea.

Kang Chol-hwan and Pierre Rigoulot. Translated by Yair Reiner. *The Aquariums of Pyongyang: Ten Years in a North Korean Gulag.* New York: Basic Books, 2001.
This memoir by a former political prisoner provides an important look into the nation's life and its violations of human rights.

McCormack, Gavan. *Target North Korea: Pushing North Korea to the Brink of Nuclear Catastrophe.* New York: Nation Books, 2004.
This book, by a professor of Pacific and Asian Studies, examines North Korea's past and present and suggests that, while the nation has genuine problems, its image has also been distorted by outside media and attitudes.

Nahm, Andrew C. "The Democratic People's Republic of Korea: History." *Regional Surveys of the World: The Far East and Australasia.* London: Europa Publications, 2002.
This article surveys the events of recent North Korean history.

Nanchu, with Xing Hang. *In North Korea: An American Travels through an Imprisoned Nation.* **Jefferson, NC: McFarland, 2003.**
This rare look at Korea through the eyes of a Chinese American traveler provides information on life in Pyongyang, the personality cult surrounding the Kims, the rising number of defectors, and other facets of the nation.

Natsios, Andrew S. *The Great North Korean Famine: Famine, Politics, and Foreign Policy.* **Washington, DC: United States Institute of Peace Press, 2001.**
This study of North Korea's famine of the late 1990s investigates its causes and effects, as well as examining its political and social meaning.

New York Times Company. *The New York Times on the Web.* **2004.**
 <www.nytimes.com> **(April 23, 2004).**
This on-line version of the newspaper offers current news stories along with an archive of articles on North Korea.

"PRB 2003 World Population Data Sheet." *Population Reference Bureau (PRB).* **2003.**
<http://www.prb.org> **(April 22, 2004).**
This annual statistics sheet provides a wealth of data on North Korea's population, birth and death rates, fertility rate, infant mortality rate, and other useful demographic information.

Savada, Andrea Matles, ed. *North Korea: A Country Study.* **Washington, DC: Federal Research Division, 1994.**
This title gives a moderately detailed overview of North Korea's history, society, government, and economy.

Turner, Barry, ed. *The Statesman's Yearbook: The Politics, Cultures, and Economies of the World, 2003.* **New York: Macmillan Press, 2002.**
This resource provides concise information on North Korean history, climate, government, economy, and culture, including relevant statistics.

BBC News. *Country Profile: North Korea.*
<http://news.bbc.co.uk/2/hi/asia-pacific/country_profiles/1131421.stm>
The BBC presents an overview of the DPRK.

Center for Nonproliferation Studies. *North Korea Special Collection*
<http://cns.miis.edu/research/korea/>
This site presents a wealth of information on North Korea's nuclear program and the crisis, including maps and satellite photos.

Chung, Okwha, and Judy Monroe. *Cooking the Korean Way.*
Minneapolis: Lerner Publications Company, 2003.
This cultural cookbook presents recipes for a variety of authentic and traditional Korean dishes, including special foods for holidays and festivals.

Feldman, Ruth Tenzer. *The Korean War.* **Minneapolis: Lerner Publications Company, 2004.**
This book presents a history of the Korean War, which tore the peninsula apart between 1950 and 1953.

Gangwon Cyber DMZ. *Korea DMZ.*
<http://www.korea-dmz.com/en/cm/main_en.asp>
This site offers a wealth of information on the Demilitarized Zone separating North and South Korea, from history and geography to wildlife.

Kim Dong-sung, ill. *Long Long Time Ago: Korean Folk Tales.*
Elizabeth, NJ: Hollym, 1997.
This illustrated collection brings together twenty traditional stories that have been loved by Korean children for generations.

Korean Central News Agency.
<http://www.kcna.co.jp/index-e.htm>
As the official news source of the DPRK, the Korean Central News Agency (KCNA) offers a look at the public face of North Korea. While the articles are often filled with propaganda, they also offer a glimpse into the government and the KWP and the images that they hope to project.

Koreascope. *North Korea Today.*
<http://www.koreascope.org/ks/eng/index.jsp>
This site, which is part of a larger site covering both Koreas, focuses on the North and its government.

Korea Web Weekly. *DPRK: Democratic People's Republic of Korea.*
<http://www.kimsoft.com/dprk.htm>
This collection of links provides many jumping-off points for learning more about North Korea.

Park, Linda Sue. *Seesaw Girl.* **New York: Clarion Books, 1999.**
The story of Jade Blossom, a girl in seventeenth-century Korea, gives readers an up-close glimpse of Korean life at the time.

———. *A Single Shard.* **New York: Clarion Books, 2001.**
This Newbery Medal-winning novel for young adults centers on Tree, an orphaned Korean boy growing up in the 1100s.

Further Reading and Websites

———. *When My Name Was Keoko.* New York: Clarion Books, 2002.
A brother and sister in Korea struggle with life under Japanese rule, during which both of them are forced to change their names.

Sherman, Josepha. *The Cold War.* Minneapolis: Lerner Publications Company, 2004.
This book introduces readers to the causes, incidents, and effects of the Cold War.

Sook Nyul Choi. *Year of Impossible Goodbyes.* Boston: Houghton Mifflin, 1991.
In this young adult novel, readers meet Sookan, a girl growing up in North Korea in 1945. Great changes are taking place: World War II is ending, as is Japanese occupation, but Soviet soldiers are taking the place of the Japanese, bringing their own rules.

vgsbooks.com
<http://www.vgsbooks.com>
Visit vgsbooks.com, the homepage of the Visual Geography Series®. You can get linked to all sorts of useful on-line information, including geographical, historical, demographic, cultural, and economic websites. The vgsbooks.com site is a great resource for late-breaking news and statistics.

Captions for photos appearing on cover and chapter openers:

Cover: A sculpture in Pyongyang, North Korea's capital, represents the value of industry to North Korea. This statue stands near the Tower of the Juche Idea, a 558-foot-high (170-m) monument to Kim Il Sung's concept of self-reliance.

pp. 4–5 Nampo residents celebrate the fiftieth anniversary of the founding of the Korean Workers' Party (KWP). Large portraits of Kim Il Sung *(second from right)*, North Korea's first leader following the division of the Korea Peninsula after World War II, and his son Kim Jong-il *(right)*, who became the leader of North Korea in 1997, are prominently displayed.

pp. 8–9 Farmers grow crops on every bit of level land available in North Korea.

pp. 18–19 Ancient musicians appear ready to perform in this fourteenth-century mural from the Tomb of King Kongmin. In modern times, the mural is displayed in the Koryo Museum—itself a sixth-century Confucian academy—in Kaesung.

pp. 38–39 Pyongyang residents attending a state holiday procession wave bouquets of flowers at the photographer.

pp. 48–49 The Pohyon Temple in the Myohyang Mountains houses an elaborate Buddhist shrine, first built in 1042. In modern times, restoration work at the site has been done as part of North Korea's annual "month of protection of cultural relics" each April.

Photo Acknowledgments
The images in this book are used with the permission of: © Art Directors/Jane Sweeney, pp. 4–5, 8–9, 16, 17, 18–19, 38–39, 41, 42, 46, 48–49, 62; © Digital Cartographics, pp. 6, 11; © Jean Chung/CORBIS, p. 12; © D. Roberts & Lorri Franz/CORBIS, p. 15; Korean Overseas Information Service, pp. 20, 23; California Academy of Sciences, p. 22; Library of Congress, p. 25 (LC-USZ62-72798); © Bettmann/CORBIS, p. 27; © Underwood Photo Archives/SuperStock, p. 29; © Hutchison Library/Trevor Page, p. 31; © SuperStock, p. 32; © Reuters/CORBIS, pp. 35, 47; © Getty Images, p. 36; © Gerald Bourke/World Food Programme/Reuters/CORBIS, p. 43; © Yokota Victoria/CORBIS SYGMA, pp. 51, 61; © Réunion des Musées Nationaux/Art Resource, NY, p. 54; © Kim Kyung-Hoon/Reuters/Landov, p. 57; Audrius Tomonis/www.banknotes.com, p. 68 (All)

Cover: © Ozcan Yuksek/Atlas. Back Cover photo: NASA